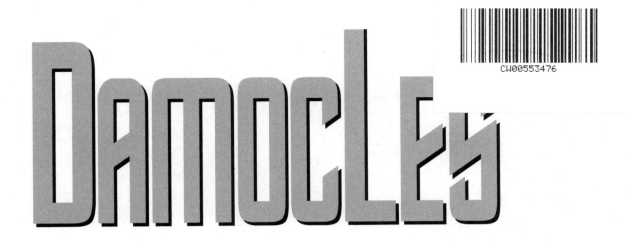

Damocles

ARTWORK: ALAIN HENRIET
SCRIPT: CALLÈDE
COLOURS: USAGI

3. PERFECT CHILD

9th CINEBOOK
The 9th Art Publisher

Original title: Damocles – Perfect Child

Original edition: © Dupuis, 2011 by Henriet & Callède
www.dupuis.com
All rights reserved

English translation: © 2015 Cinebook Ltd

Translator: Mark Bence
Lettering and text layout: Design Amorandi
Printed in Spain by EGEDSA

This edition first published in Great Britain in 2016 by
Cinebook Ltd
56 Beech Avenue
Canterbury, Kent
CT4 7TA
www.cinebook.com

A CIP catalogue record for this book
is available from the British Library

ISBN 978-1-84918-279-9

9th CINEBOOK
The 9th Art Publisher

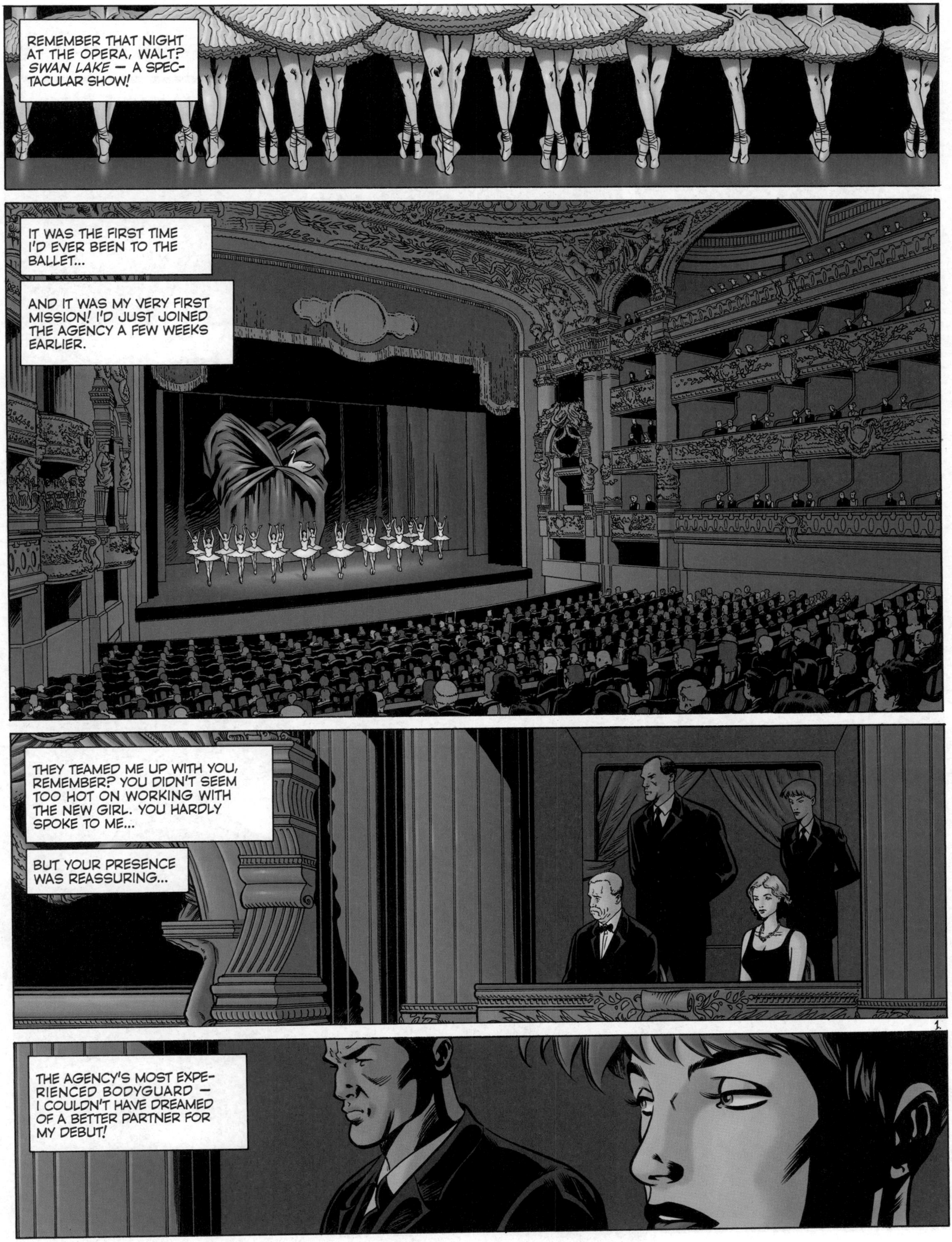
REMEMBER THAT NIGHT AT THE OPERA, WALT? *SWAN LAKE* — A SPECTACULAR SHOW!
IT WAS THE FIRST TIME I'D EVER BEEN TO THE BALLET...
AND IT WAS MY VERY FIRST MISSION! I'D JUST JOINED THE AGENCY A FEW WEEKS EARLIER.
THEY TEAMED ME UP WITH YOU, REMEMBER? YOU DIDN'T SEEM TOO HOT ON WORKING WITH THE NEW GIRL. YOU HARDLY SPOKE TO ME...
BUT YOUR PRESENCE WAS REASSURING...
THE AGENCY'S MOST EXPERIENCED BODYGUARD — I COULDN'T HAVE DREAMED OF A BETTER PARTNER FOR MY DEBUT!

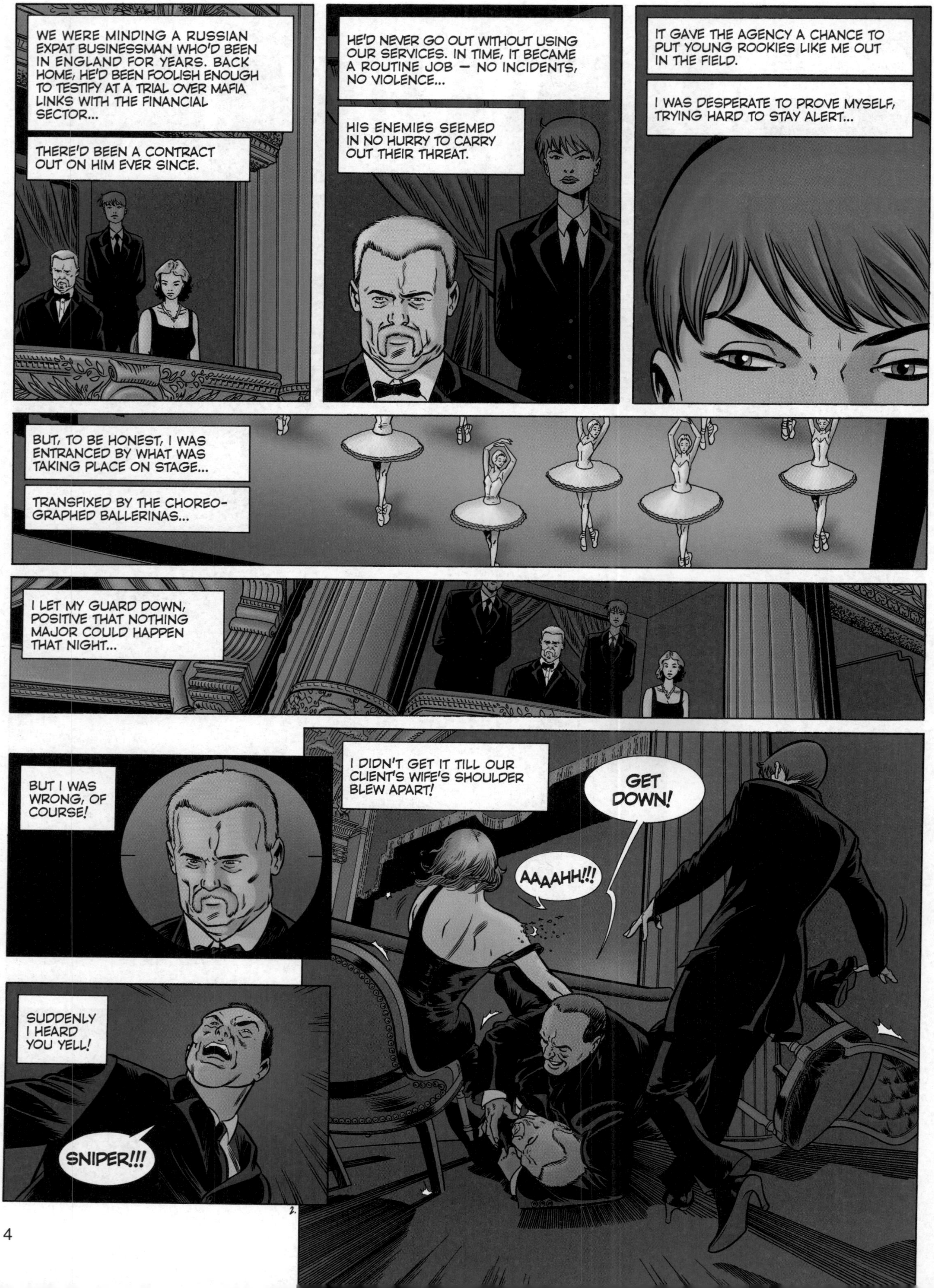
WE WERE MINDING A RUSSIAN EXPAT BUSINESSMAN WHO'D BEEN IN ENGLAND FOR YEARS. BACK HOME, HE'D BEEN FOOLISH ENOUGH TO TESTIFY AT A TRIAL OVER MAFIA LINKS WITH THE FINANCIAL SECTOR...
THERE'D BEEN A CONTRACT OUT ON HIM EVER SINCE.
HE'D NEVER GO OUT WITHOUT USING OUR SERVICES. IN TIME, IT BECAME A ROUTINE JOB — NO INCIDENTS, NO VIOLENCE...
HIS ENEMIES SEEMED IN NO HURRY TO CARRY OUT THEIR THREAT.
IT GAVE THE AGENCY A CHANCE TO PUT YOUNG ROOKIES LIKE ME OUT IN THE FIELD.
I WAS DESPERATE TO PROVE MYSELF, TRYING HARD TO STAY ALERT...
BUT, TO BE HONEST, I WAS ENTRANCED BY WHAT WAS TAKING PLACE ON STAGE...
TRANSFIXED BY THE CHOREO-GRAPHED BALLERINAS...
I LET MY GUARD DOWN, POSITIVE THAT NOTHING MAJOR COULD HAPPEN THAT NIGHT...
BUT I WAS WRONG, OF COURSE!
I DIDN'T GET IT TILL OUR CLIENT'S WIFE'S SHOULDER BLEW APART!
GET DOWN!
AAAAHH!!!
SUDDENLY I HEARD YOU YELL!
SNIPER!!!

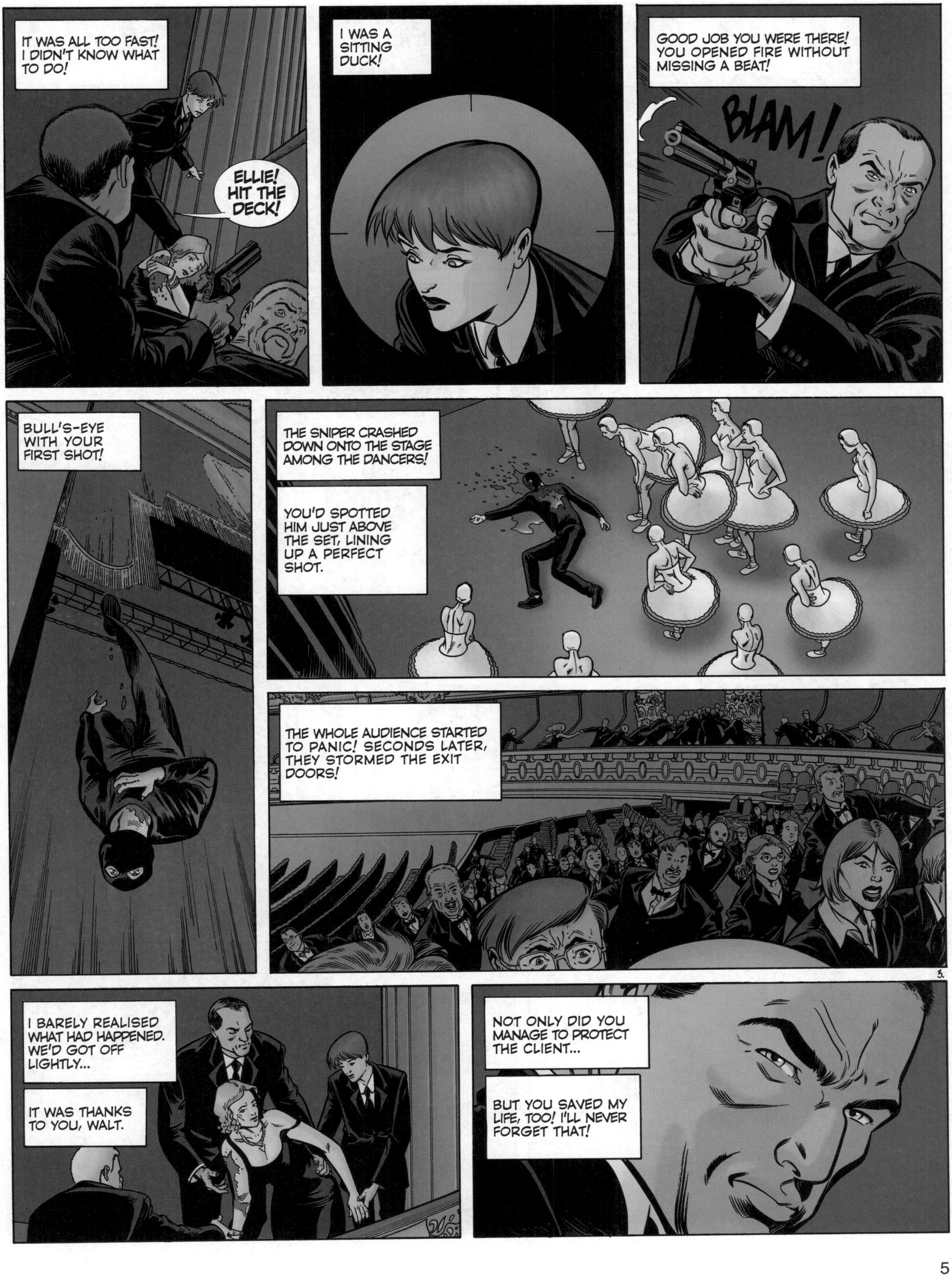
IT WAS ALL TOO FAST! I DIDN'T KNOW WHAT TO DO!
ELLIE! HIT THE DECK!
I WAS A SITTING DUCK!
GOOD JOB YOU WERE THERE! YOU OPENED FIRE WITHOUT MISSING A BEAT!
BLAM!
BULL'S-EYE WITH YOUR FIRST SHOT!
THE SNIPER CRASHED DOWN ONTO THE STAGE AMONG THE DANCERS!
YOU'D SPOTTED HIM JUST ABOVE THE SET, LINING UP A PERFECT SHOT.
THE WHOLE AUDIENCE STARTED TO PANIC! SECONDS LATER, THEY STORMED THE EXIT DOORS!
I BARELY REALISED WHAT HAD HAPPENED. WE'D GOT OFF LIGHTLY...
IT WAS THANKS TO YOU, WALT.
NOT ONLY DID YOU MANAGE TO PROTECT THE CLIENT...
BUT YOU SAVED MY LIFE, TOO! I'LL NEVER FORGET THAT!

SINCE THAT FIRST MISSION, I'VE ALWAYS TRUSTED YOU IMPLICITLY...

KNOWING YOU'D BE THERE TO WATCH OVER ME.

YOU CAN'T JUST LEAVE ME, WALT... YOU KNOW I NEED YOU!

I BEG YOU, YOU CAN'T GIVE UP NOW.

YOU'LL PULL THROUGH. FIGHT IT!!! YOU WERE ALWAYS THE BEST!

I PROMISE I'LL BE HERE WHEN YOU COME ROUND! THEN IT'LL BE MY TURN TO WATCH OVER YOU...

I HAVE TO ADMIRE YOUR DEVOTION, MISS BRAXTON.

YOU COME NEARLY EVERY NIGHT, AND YOU'RE ONE OF THE FEW PEOPLE WHO VISIT HIM AT ALL.

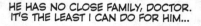

HE HAS NO CLOSE FAMILY, DOCTOR. IT'S THE LEAST I CAN DO FOR HIM...

YOU'RE RIGHT TO TALK TO HIM. IT'S IMPORTANT TO KEEP COMA PATIENTS STIMULATED.

IT'S NOT HAVING MUCH EFFECT, SADLY...

YOUR COLLEAGUE SUFFERED A VIOLENT INJURY. IT'S A MIRACLE HE'S STILL ALIVE...

YOU'LL HAVE TO BE PATIENT.

IT'S ALL SO FRUSTRATING, JUST WAITING HERE, POWERLESS!

I SO WISH I COULD HELP HIM...

4.

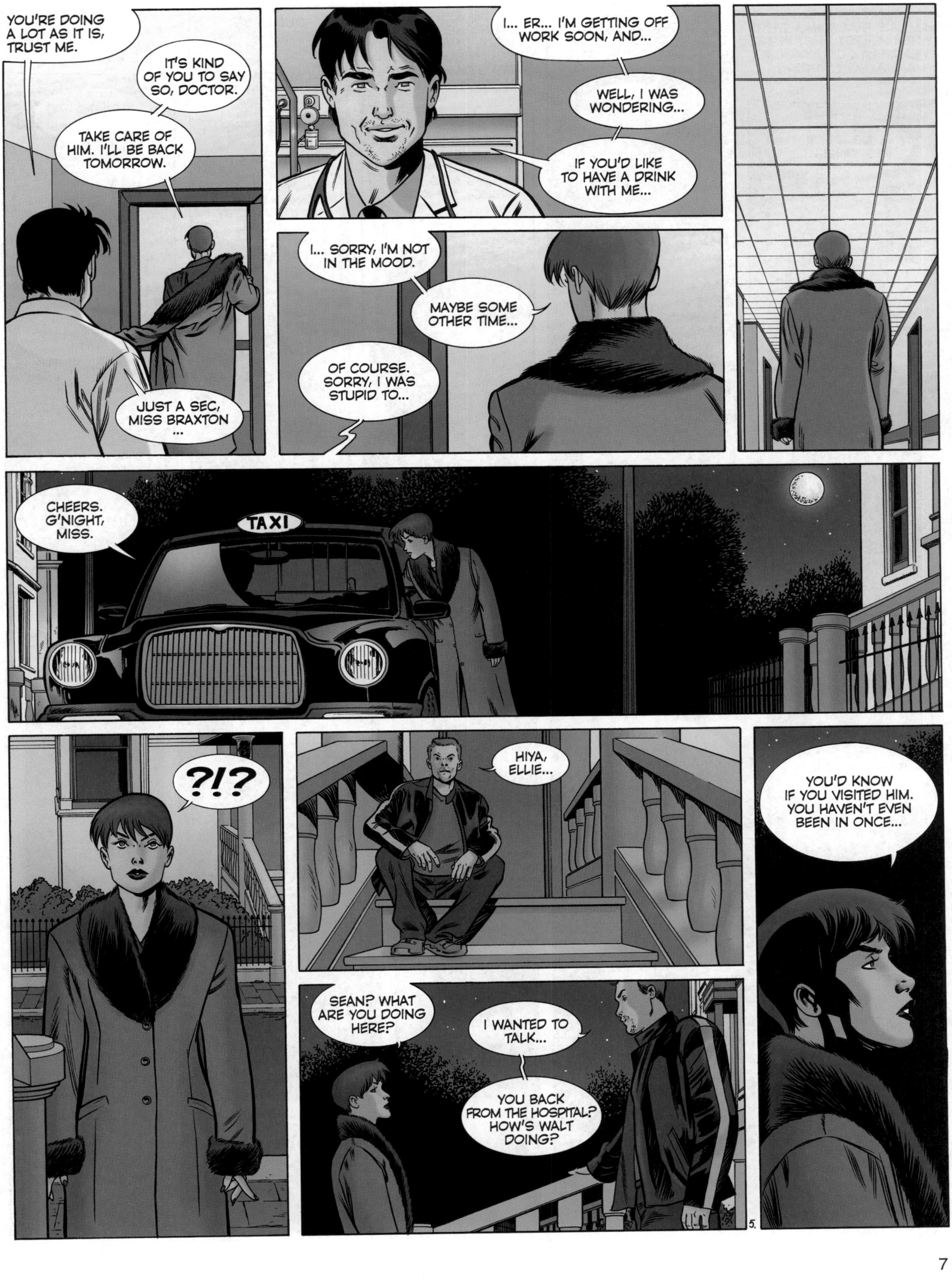
YOU'RE DOING A LOT AS IT IS, TRUST ME.
IT'S KIND OF YOU TO SAY SO, DOCTOR.
TAKE CARE OF HIM. I'LL BE BACK TOMORROW.
JUST A SEC, MISS BRAXTON ...
I... ER... I'M GETTING OFF WORK SOON, AND...
WELL, I WAS WONDERING...
IF YOU'D LIKE TO HAVE A DRINK WITH ME...
I... SORRY, I'M NOT IN THE MOOD.
MAYBE SOME OTHER TIME...
OF COURSE. SORRY, I WAS STUPID TO...
CHEERS. G'NIGHT, MISS.
TAXI
?!?
HIYA, ELLIE...
SEAN? WHAT ARE YOU DOING HERE?
I WANTED TO TALK...
YOU BACK FROM THE HOSPITAL? HOW'S WALT DOING?
YOU'D KNOW IF YOU VISITED HIM. YOU HAVEN'T EVEN BEEN IN ONCE...
5.

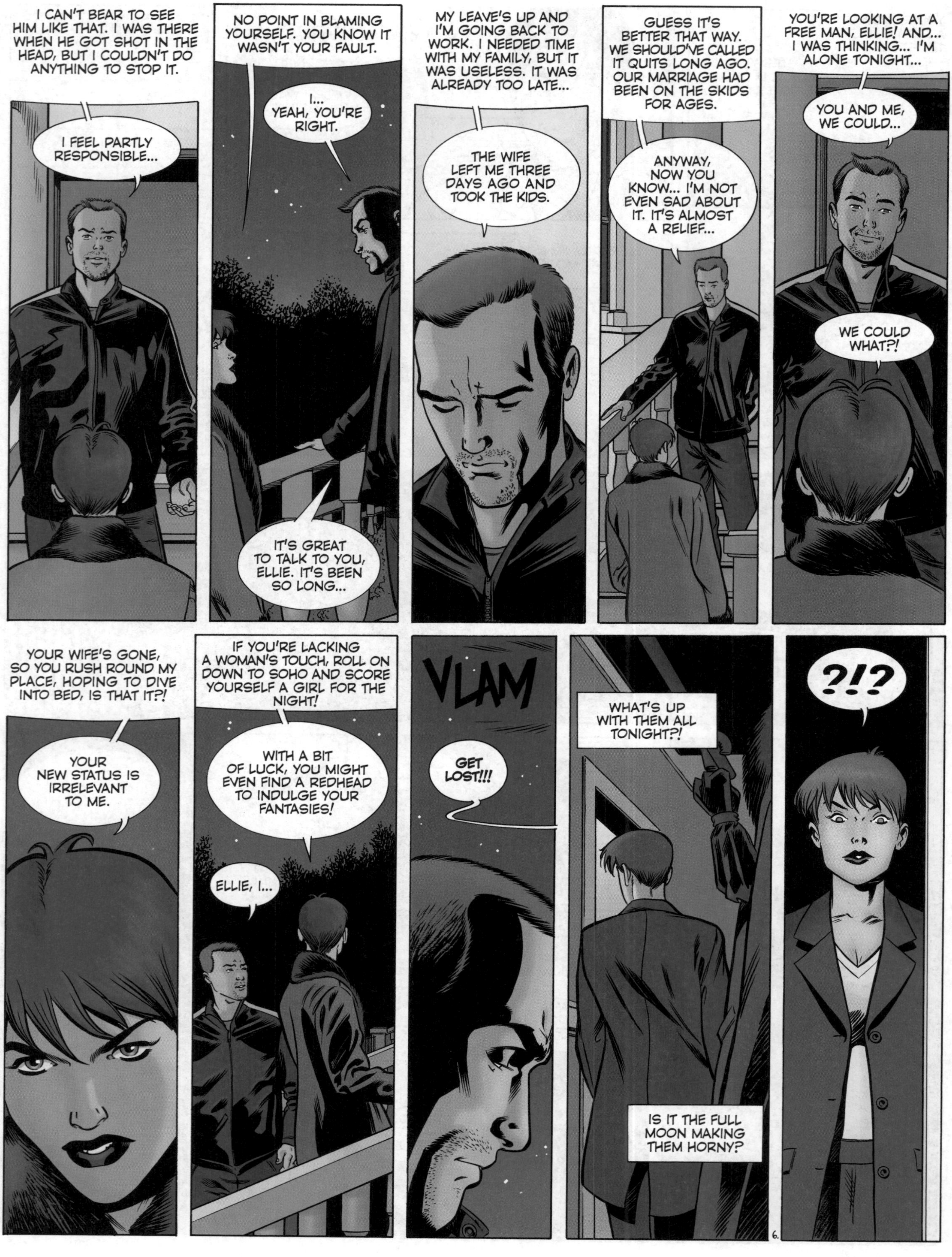
I CAN'T BEAR TO SEE HIM LIKE THAT. I WAS THERE WHEN HE GOT SHOT IN THE HEAD, BUT I COULDN'T DO ANYTHING TO STOP IT.
I FEEL PARTLY RESPONSIBLE...
NO POINT IN BLAMING YOURSELF. YOU KNOW IT WASN'T YOUR FAULT.
I... YEAH, YOU'RE RIGHT.
IT'S GREAT TO TALK TO YOU, ELLIE. IT'S BEEN SO LONG...
MY LEAVE'S UP AND I'M GOING BACK TO WORK. I NEEDED TIME WITH MY FAMILY, BUT IT WAS USELESS. IT WAS ALREADY TOO LATE...
THE WIFE LEFT ME THREE DAYS AGO AND TOOK THE KIDS.
GUESS IT'S BETTER THAT WAY. WE SHOULD'VE CALLED IT QUITS LONG AGO. OUR MARRIAGE HAD BEEN ON THE SKIDS FOR AGES.
ANYWAY, NOW YOU KNOW... I'M NOT EVEN SAD ABOUT IT. IT'S ALMOST A RELIEF...
YOU'RE LOOKING AT A FREE MAN, ELLIE! AND... I WAS THINKING... I'M ALONE TONIGHT...
YOU AND ME, WE COULD...
WE COULD WHAT?!
YOUR WIFE'S GONE, SO YOU RUSH ROUND MY PLACE, HOPING TO DIVE INTO BED, IS THAT IT?!
YOUR NEW STATUS IS IRRELEVANT TO ME.
IF YOU'RE LACKING A WOMAN'S TOUCH, ROLL ON DOWN TO SOHO AND SCORE YOURSELF A GIRL FOR THE NIGHT!
WITH A BIT OF LUCK, YOU MIGHT EVEN FIND A REDHEAD TO INDULGE YOUR FANTASIES!
ELLIE, I...
VLAM
GET LOST!!!
WHAT'S UP WITH THEM ALL TONIGHT?!
IS IT THE FULL MOON MAKING THEM HORNY?
?!?
6.

OH, ELLIE!!! I... UM... HAD A NICE DAY?

THIS IS BRAD, AND...

ER... HI THERE...

OK, LET'S PRETEND I NEVER SAW THIS...

I'M OFF UP TO BED. DO TRY NOT TO BE TOO NOISY...

MMMHH... YES! YES!! BRAD!!!

OOOOOHHH!!!

SOUNDS LIKE IT'S FINALLY OVER... SOME STAYING POWER, THAT BRAD!

HAD TO PUT UP WITH THEIR MOANING FOR HOURS... I'M NOT EVEN TIRED ANY MORE.

MAYBE I SHOULD THINK OF MOVING OUT? WE'VE GOT TOTALLY DIFFERENT LIFESTYLES, DIANA AND ME.

AND IT'S HARD TO GET ANY PRIVACY WHEN SHE KEEPS BRINGING GUYS HOME.

ONE THING'S FOR SURE: HER SEX LIFE'S ENERGETIC... MORE THAN CAN BE SAID OF MINE!

CAN'T RECALL WHEN I LAST SLEPT WITH A GUY, AND IT'S UNLIKELY TO CHANGE IF I PUSH AWAY EVERYONE WHO FANCIES ME...

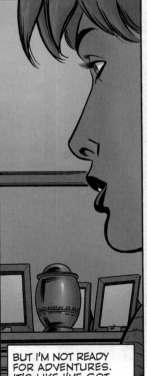

BUT I'M NOT READY FOR ADVENTURES. IT'S LIKE I'VE GOT SOME KIND OF INNER FIREWALL.

I KNOW WHAT'S WRONG...

THERE'S SOME-ONE IN MY LIFE ALREADY...

AND HIS MEMORY TAKES UP WAY TOO MUCH ROOM.

JUST FACE IT, HON — YOU'RE STILL GRIEVING FOR YOUR FATHER.

A SHRINK WOULD HAVE A BALL WITH YOU...

7.

9

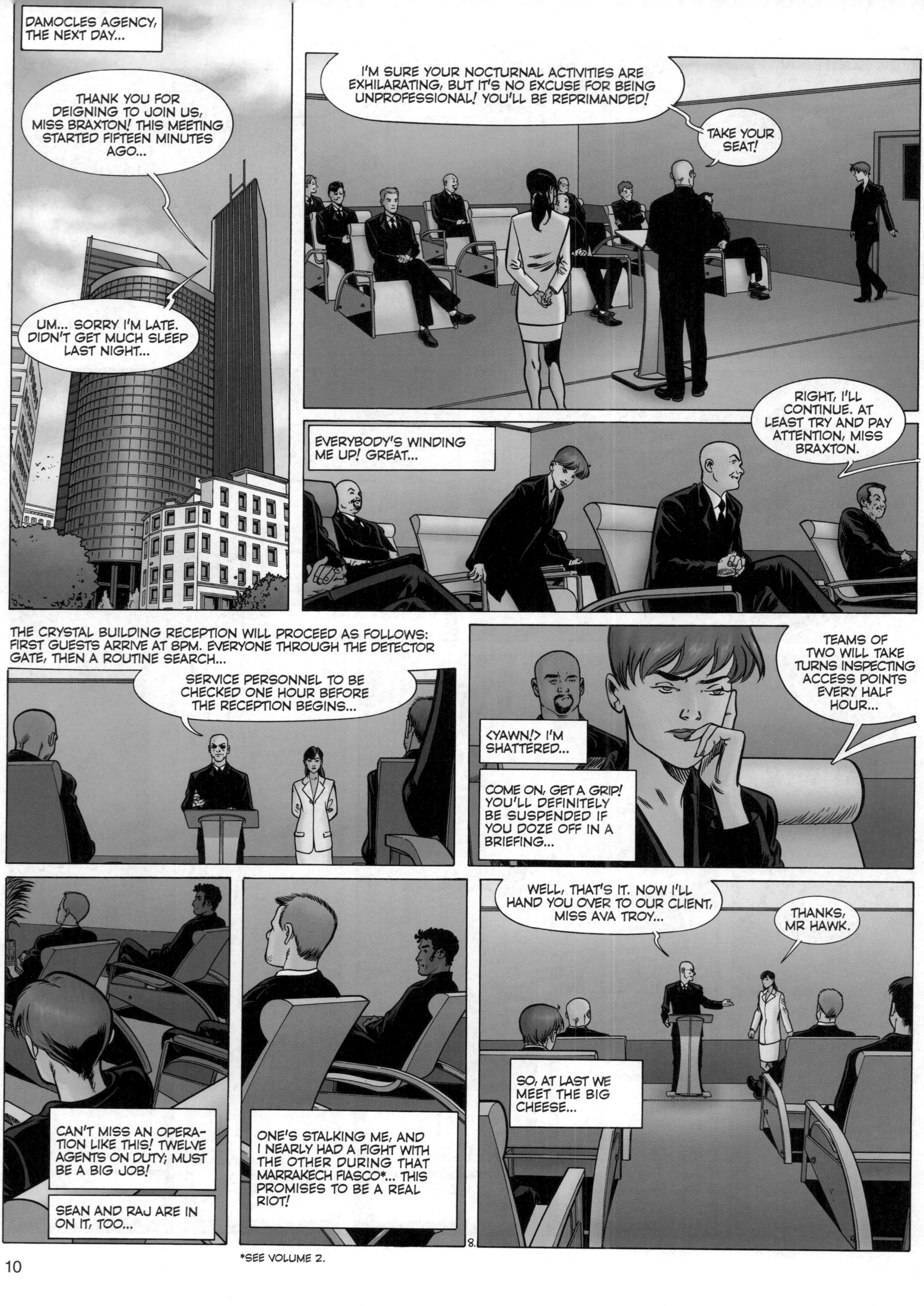

DAMOCLES AGENCY, THE NEXT DAY...
THANK YOU FOR DEIGNING TO JOIN US, MISS BRAXTON! THIS MEETING STARTED FIFTEEN MINUTES AGO...
UM... SORRY I'M LATE. DIDN'T GET MUCH SLEEP LAST NIGHT...
I'M SURE YOUR NOCTURNAL ACTIVITIES ARE EXHILARATING, BUT IT'S NO EXCUSE FOR BEING UNPROFESSIONAL! YOU'LL BE REPRIMANDED!
TAKE YOUR SEAT!
EVERYBODY'S WINDING ME UP! GREAT...
RIGHT, I'LL CONTINUE. AT LEAST TRY AND PAY ATTENTION, MISS BRAXTON.
THE CRYSTAL BUILDING RECEPTION WILL PROCEED AS FOLLOWS: FIRST GUESTS ARRIVE AT 8PM. EVERYONE THROUGH THE DETECTOR GATE, THEN A ROUTINE SEARCH...
SERVICE PERSONNEL TO BE CHECKED ONE HOUR BEFORE THE RECEPTION BEGINS...
TEAMS OF TWO WILL TAKE TURNS INSPECTING ACCESS POINTS EVERY HALF HOUR...
<YAWN!> I'M SHATTERED...
COME ON, GET A GRIP! YOU'LL DEFINITELY BE SUSPENDED IF YOU DOZE OFF IN A BRIEFING...
CAN'T MISS AN OPERATION LIKE THIS! TWELVE AGENTS ON DUTY; MUST BE A BIG JOB!
SEAN AND RAJ ARE IN ON IT, TOO...
ONE'S STALKING ME, AND I NEARLY HAD A FIGHT WITH THE OTHER DURING THAT MARRAKECH FIASCO*... THIS PROMISES TO BE A REAL RIOT!
WELL, THAT'S IT. NOW I'LL HAND YOU OVER TO OUR CLIENT, MISS AVA TROY...
THANKS, MR HAWK.
SO, AT LAST WE MEET THE BIG CHEESE...
8.

*SEE VOLUME 2.

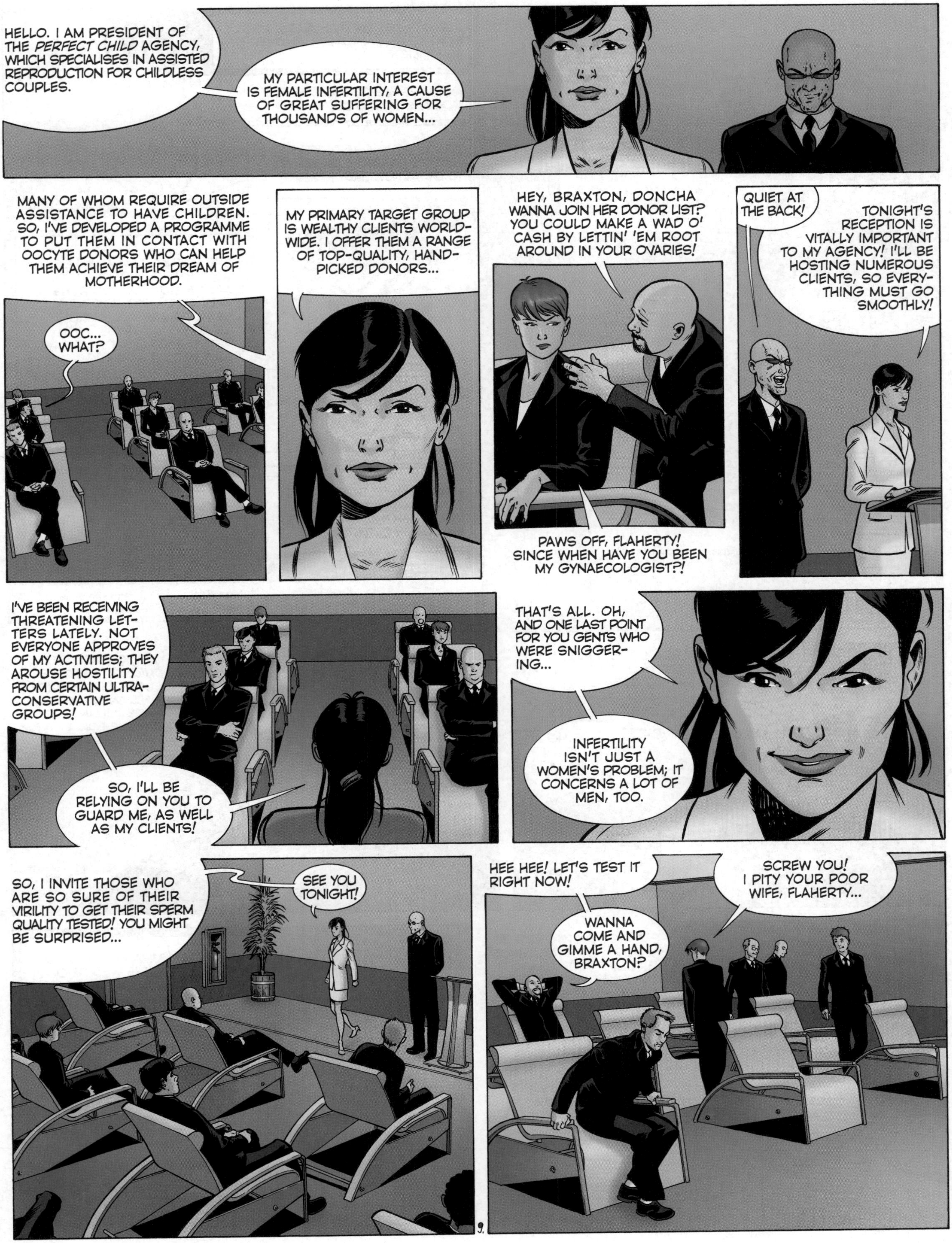
HELLO. I AM PRESIDENT OF THE *PERFECT CHILD* AGENCY, WHICH SPECIALISES IN ASSISTED REPRODUCTION FOR CHILDLESS COUPLES.
MY PARTICULAR INTEREST IS FEMALE INFERTILITY, A CAUSE OF GREAT SUFFERING FOR THOUSANDS OF WOMEN...
MANY OF WHOM REQUIRE OUTSIDE ASSISTANCE TO HAVE CHILDREN. SO, I'VE DEVELOPED A PROGRAMME TO PUT THEM IN CONTACT WITH OOCYTE DONORS WHO CAN HELP THEM ACHIEVE THEIR DREAM OF MOTHERHOOD.
OOC... WHAT?
MY PRIMARY TARGET GROUP IS WEALTHY CLIENTS WORLD-WIDE. I OFFER THEM A RANGE OF TOP-QUALITY, HAND-PICKED DONORS...
HEY, BRAXTON, DONCHA WANNA JOIN HER DONOR LIST? YOU COULD MAKE A WAD O' CASH BY LETTIN' 'EM ROOT AROUND IN YOUR OVARIES!
PAWS OFF, FLAHERTY! SINCE WHEN HAVE YOU BEEN MY GYNAECOLOGIST?!
QUIET AT THE BACK!
TONIGHT'S RECEPTION IS VITALLY IMPORTANT TO MY AGENCY! I'LL BE HOSTING NUMEROUS CLIENTS, SO EVERY-THING MUST GO SMOOTHLY!
I'VE BEEN RECEIVING THREATENING LET-TERS LATELY. NOT EVERYONE APPROVES OF MY ACTIVITIES; THEY AROUSE HOSTILITY FROM CERTAIN ULTRA-CONSERVATIVE GROUPS!
SO, I'LL BE RELYING ON YOU TO GUARD ME, AS WELL AS MY CLIENTS!
THAT'S ALL. OH, AND ONE LAST POINT FOR YOU GENTS WHO WERE SNIGGER-ING...
INFERTILITY ISN'T JUST A WOMEN'S PROBLEM; IT CONCERNS A LOT OF MEN, TOO.
SO, I INVITE THOSE WHO ARE SO SURE OF THEIR VIRILITY TO GET THEIR SPERM QUALITY TESTED! YOU MIGHT BE SURPRISED...
SEE YOU TONIGHT!
HEE HEE! LET'S TEST IT RIGHT NOW!
WANNA COME AND GIMME A HAND, BRAXTON?
SCREW YOU! I PITY YOUR POOR WIFE, FLAHERTY...
9.

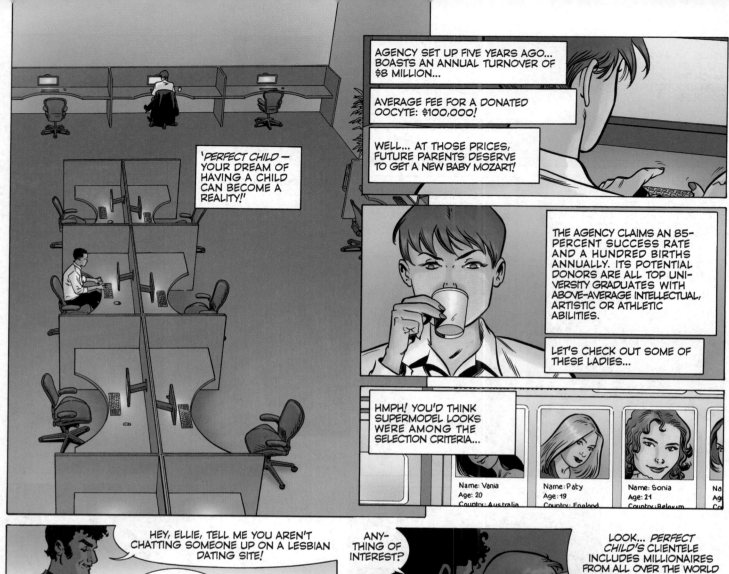

AGENCY SET UP FIVE YEARS AGO... BOASTS AN ANNUAL TURNOVER OF $8 MILLION...

AVERAGE FEE FOR A DONATED OOCYTE: $100,000!

WELL... AT THOSE PRICES, FUTURE PARENTS DESERVE TO GET A NEW BABY MOZART!

'PERFECT CHILD — YOUR DREAM OF HAVING A CHILD CAN BECOME A REALITY!'

THE AGENCY CLAIMS AN 85-PERCENT SUCCESS RATE AND A HUNDRED BIRTHS ANNUALLY. ITS POTENTIAL DONORS ARE ALL TOP UNIVERSITY GRADUATES WITH ABOVE-AVERAGE INTELLECTUAL, ARTISTIC OR ATHLETIC ABILITIES.

LET'S CHECK OUT SOME OF THESE LADIES...

HMPH! YOU'D THINK SUPERMODEL LOOKS WERE AMONG THE SELECTION CRITERIA...

Name: Vania
Age: 20
Country: Australia

Name: Paty
Age: 19
Country: England

Name: Sonia
Age: 21
Country: Belgium

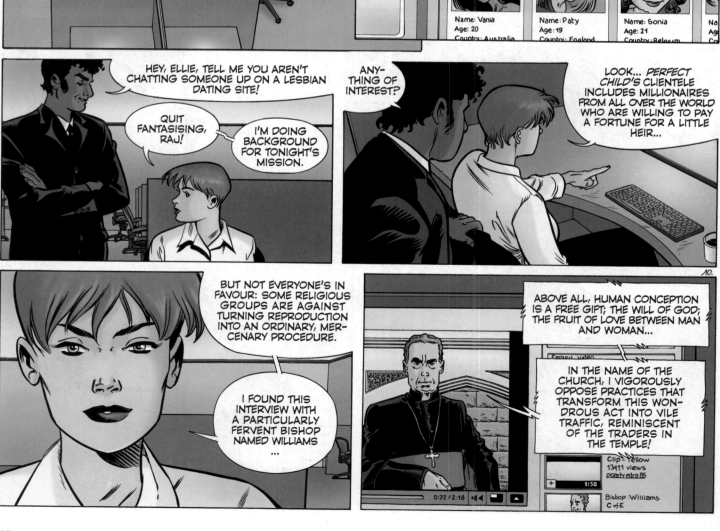

HEY, ELLIE, TELL ME YOU AREN'T CHATTING SOMEONE UP ON A LESBIAN DATING SITE!

QUIT FANTASISING, RAJ!

I'M DOING BACKGROUND FOR TONIGHT'S MISSION.

ANY-THING OF INTEREST?

LOOK... PERFECT CHILD'S CLIENTELE INCLUDES MILLIONAIRES FROM ALL OVER THE WORLD WHO ARE WILLING TO PAY A FORTUNE FOR A LITTLE HEIR...

BUT NOT EVERYONE'S IN FAVOUR: SOME RELIGIOUS GROUPS ARE AGAINST TURNING REPRODUCTION INTO AN ORDINARY, MER-CENARY PROCEDURE.

I FOUND THIS INTERVIEW WITH A PARTICULARLY FERVENT BISHOP NAMED WILLIAMS ...

ABOVE ALL, HUMAN CONCEPTION IS A FREE GIFT; THE WILL OF GOD; THE FRUIT OF LOVE BETWEEN MAN AND WOMAN...

IN THE NAME OF THE CHURCH, I VIGOROUSLY OPPOSE PRACTICES THAT TRANSFORM THIS WON-DROUS ACT INTO VILE TRAFFIC, REMINISCENT OF THE TRADERS IN THE TEMPLE!

Embed video

Clip - Yellow
13411 views
poorly edra 85

0:22 / 2:18

1:50

Bishop Williams
C of E

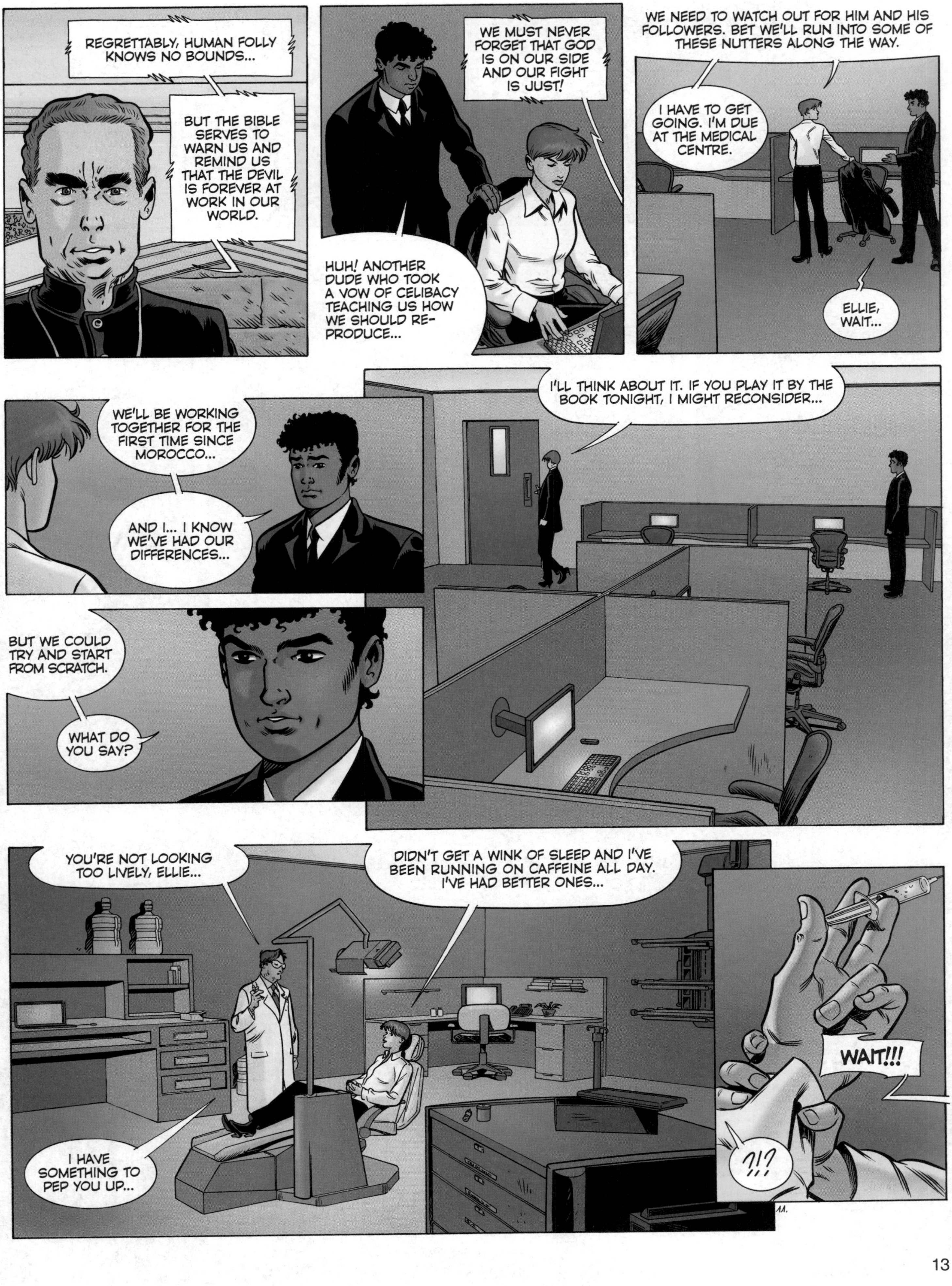
REGRETTABLY, HUMAN FOLLY KNOWS NO BOUNDS...
BUT THE BIBLE SERVES TO WARN US AND REMIND US THAT THE DEVIL IS FOREVER AT WORK IN OUR WORLD.
WE MUST NEVER FORGET THAT GOD IS ON OUR SIDE AND OUR FIGHT IS JUST!
HUH! ANOTHER DUDE WHO TOOK A VOW OF CELIBACY TEACHING US HOW WE SHOULD RE-PRODUCE...
WE NEED TO WATCH OUT FOR HIM AND HIS FOLLOWERS. BET WE'LL RUN INTO SOME OF THESE NUTTERS ALONG THE WAY.
I HAVE TO GET GOING. I'M DUE AT THE MEDICAL CENTRE.
ELLIE, WAIT...
WE'LL BE WORKING TOGETHER FOR THE FIRST TIME SINCE MOROCCO...
AND I... I KNOW WE'VE HAD OUR DIFFERENCES...
BUT WE COULD TRY AND START FROM SCRATCH.
WHAT DO YOU SAY?
I'LL THINK ABOUT IT. IF YOU PLAY IT BY THE BOOK TONIGHT, I MIGHT RECONSIDER...
YOU'RE NOT LOOKING TOO LIVELY, ELLIE...
DIDN'T GET A WINK OF SLEEP AND I'VE BEEN RUNNING ON CAFFEINE ALL DAY. I'VE HAD BETTER ONES...
I HAVE SOMETHING TO PEP YOU UP...
WAIT!!!
?!?

SORRY, DOC, BUT I ... I'M HAVING DOUBTS...

COME ON, ELLIE: A SHOT OF 'BLITZ' WILL DO YOU THE WORLD OF GOOD.

HOW CAN YOU BE SURE?

SO LITTLE IS KNOWN ABOUT THIS 'MIRACLE DRUG'... I FOUND OUT THAT ITS MANUFACTURER, EL-AHMAD GROUP, TESTS ON HUMAN GUINEA PIGS IN PRISON CAMPS.*

IT'S HARD TO CONDONE SUCH PRACTICES...

*SEE VOLUME 2.

DO YOU HAVE PROOF OF THESE CLAIMS?

I... NO, NOT REALLY.

YOU KNOW AS WELL AS I DO THAT MEDICAL RESEARCH HAS ALWAYS REQUIRED HUMAN TRIALS TO ADVANCE. THAT'S OLD NEWS...

IT'S MY JOB TO CERTIFY YOU'RE ADMINISTERED 'BLITZ' UNDER OPTIMUM CONDITIONS TO IMPROVE YOUR PERFORMANCE...

AND I'M DOING THAT...

YOU'RE FORGETTING WALT! YOUR SHOTS DIDN'T EXACTLY PROTECT HIM...

REALLY? PERHAPS THE 'BLITZ' IN HIS VEINS SAVED HIS LIFE.

OBVIOUSLY, YOU'RE FREE TO REFUSE THIS INJECTION, ELLIE...

BUT YOU'LL NO LONGER BE ELIGIBLE FOR FIELD MISSIONS. THOSE ARE THE RULES.

SO, IT'S UP TO YOU...

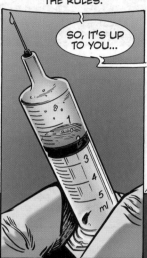

12.

THE CRYSTAL BUILDING, A FEW HOURS LATER...

CHILDREN AREN'T COMMODITIES!!!

STOP THE OOCYTE TRAFFICKING !!!

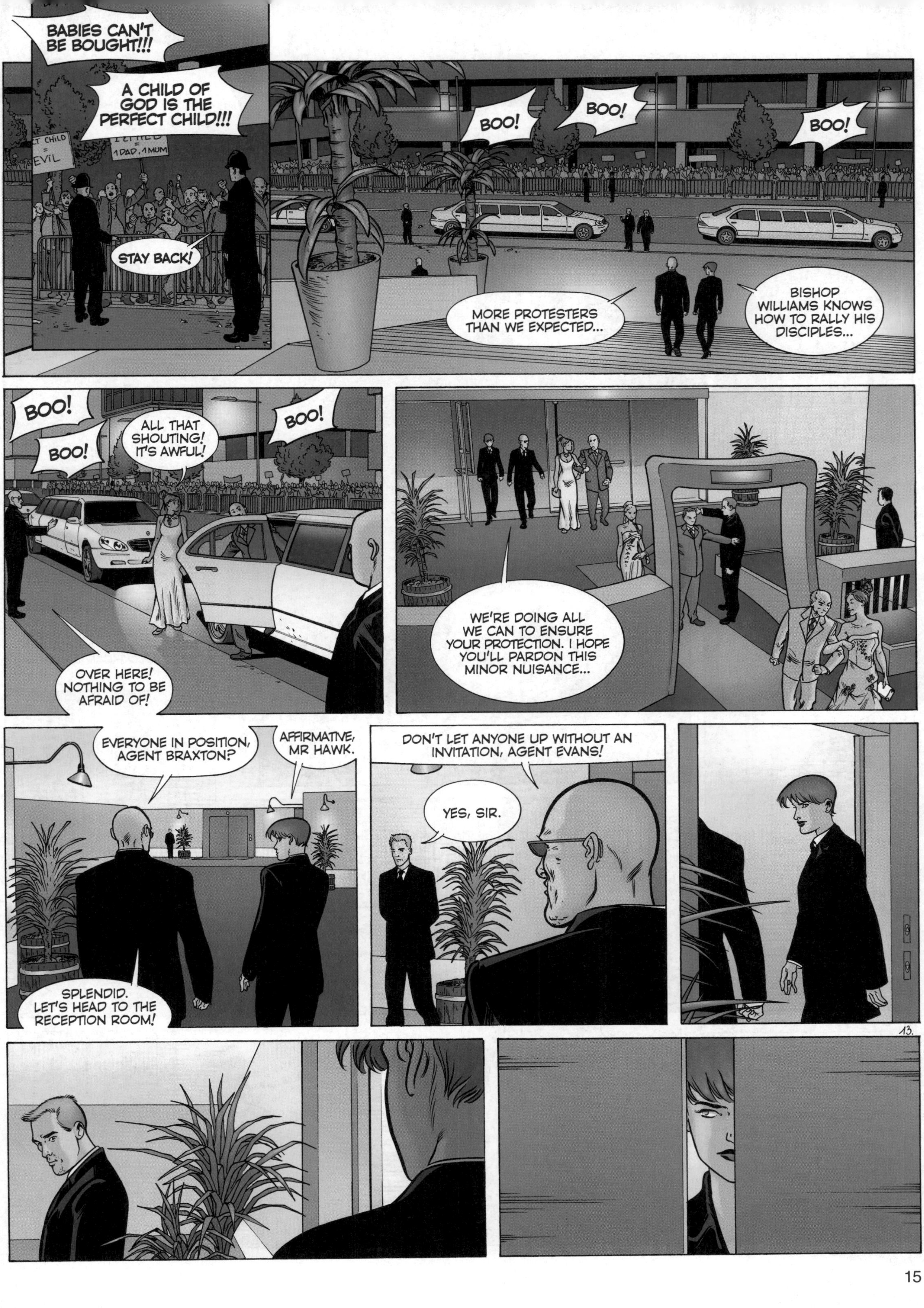
BABIES CAN'T BE BOUGHT!!!
A CHILD OF GOD IS THE PERFECT CHILD!!!
STAY BACK!
BOO!
BOO!
BOO!
MORE PROTESTERS THAN WE EXPECTED...
BISHOP WILLIAMS KNOWS HOW TO RALLY HIS DISCIPLES...
BOO!
BOO!
ALL THAT SHOUTING! IT'S AWFUL!
BOO!
OVER HERE! NOTHING TO BE AFRAID OF!
WE'RE DOING ALL WE CAN TO ENSURE YOUR PROTECTION. I HOPE YOU'LL PARDON THIS MINOR NUISANCE...
EVERYONE IN POSITION, AGENT BRAXTON?
AFFIRMATIVE, MR HAWK.
SPLENDID. LET'S HEAD TO THE RECEPTION ROOM!
DON'T LET ANYONE UP WITHOUT AN INVITATION, AGENT EVANS!
YES, SIR.
13.

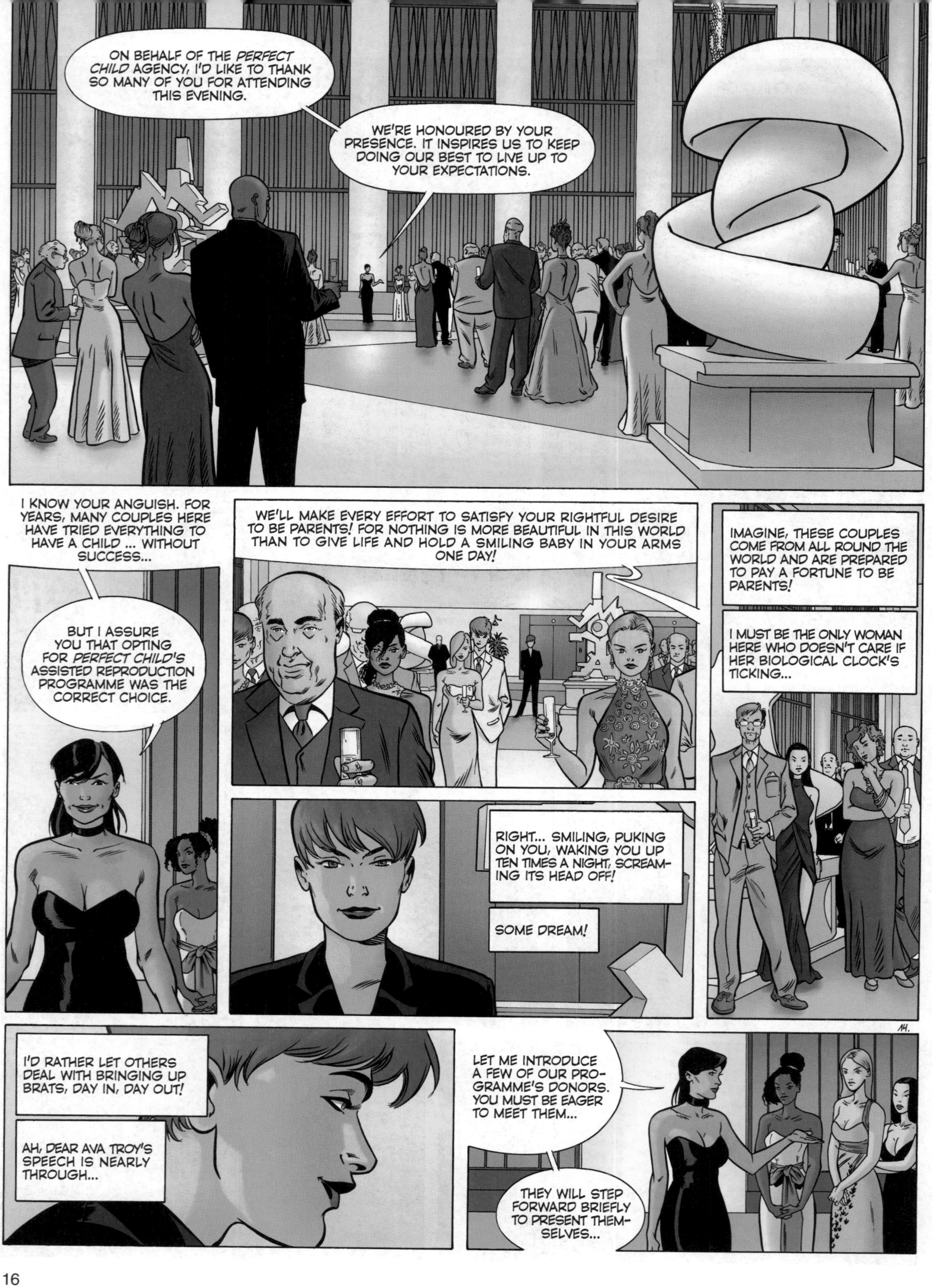

ON BEHALF OF THE *PERFECT CHILD* AGENCY, I'D LIKE TO THANK SO MANY OF YOU FOR ATTENDING THIS EVENING.
WE'RE HONOURED BY YOUR PRESENCE. IT INSPIRES US TO KEEP DOING OUR BEST TO LIVE UP TO YOUR EXPECTATIONS.
I KNOW YOUR ANGUISH. FOR YEARS, MANY COUPLES HERE HAVE TRIED EVERYTHING TO HAVE A CHILD ... WITHOUT SUCCESS...
BUT I ASSURE YOU THAT OPTING FOR *PERFECT CHILD*'S ASSISTED REPRODUCTION PROGRAMME WAS THE CORRECT CHOICE.
WE'LL MAKE EVERY EFFORT TO SATISFY YOUR RIGHTFUL DESIRE TO BE PARENTS! FOR NOTHING IS MORE BEAUTIFUL IN THIS WORLD THAN TO GIVE LIFE AND HOLD A SMILING BABY IN YOUR ARMS ONE DAY!
RIGHT... SMILING, PUKING ON YOU, WAKING YOU UP TEN TIMES A NIGHT, SCREAMING ITS HEAD OFF!
SOME DREAM!
IMAGINE, THESE COUPLES COME FROM ALL ROUND THE WORLD AND ARE PREPARED TO PAY A FORTUNE TO BE PARENTS!
I MUST BE THE ONLY WOMAN HERE WHO DOESN'T CARE IF HER BIOLOGICAL CLOCK'S TICKING...
AH.
I'D RATHER LET OTHERS DEAL WITH BRINGING UP BRATS, DAY IN, DAY OUT!
AH, DEAR AVA TROY'S SPEECH IS NEARLY THROUGH...
LET ME INTRODUCE A FEW OF OUR PROGRAMME'S DONORS. YOU MUST BE EAGER TO MEET THEM...
THEY WILL STEP FORWARD BRIEFLY TO PRESENT THEMSELVES...

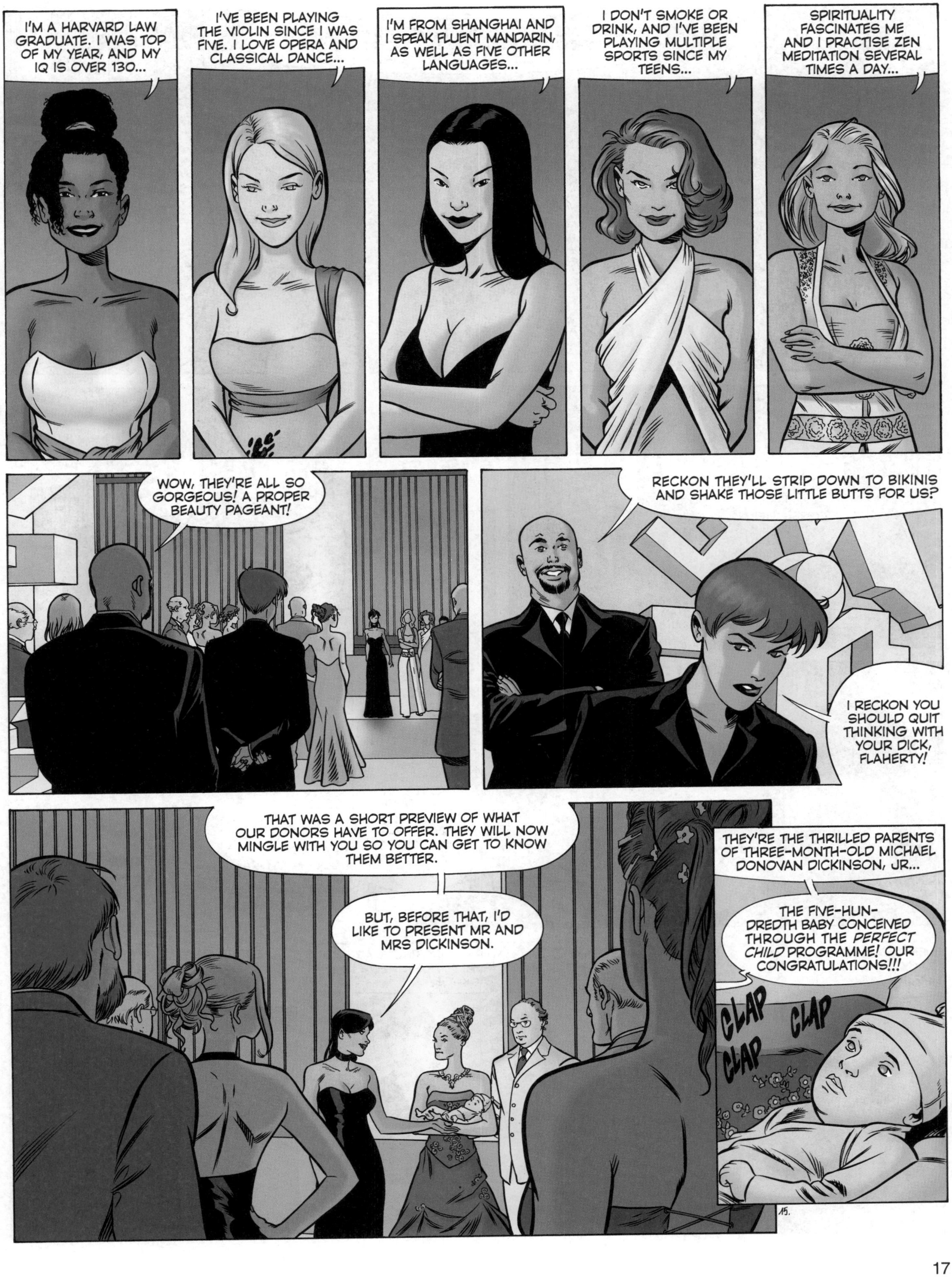

I'M A HARVARD LAW GRADUATE. I WAS TOP OF MY YEAR, AND MY IQ IS OVER 130...
I'VE BEEN PLAYING THE VIOLIN SINCE I WAS FIVE. I LOVE OPERA AND CLASSICAL DANCE...
I'M FROM SHANGHAI AND I SPEAK FLUENT MANDARIN, AS WELL AS FIVE OTHER LANGUAGES...
I DON'T SMOKE OR DRINK, AND I'VE BEEN PLAYING MULTIPLE SPORTS SINCE MY TEENS...
SPIRITUALITY FASCINATES ME AND I PRACTISE ZEN MEDITATION SEVERAL TIMES A DAY...
WOW, THEY'RE ALL SO GORGEOUS! A PROPER BEAUTY PAGEANT!
RECKON THEY'LL STRIP DOWN TO BIKINIS AND SHAKE THOSE LITTLE BUTTS FOR US?
I RECKON YOU SHOULD QUIT THINKING WITH YOUR DICK, FLAHERTY!
THAT WAS A SHORT PREVIEW OF WHAT OUR DONORS HAVE TO OFFER. THEY WILL NOW MINGLE WITH YOU SO YOU CAN GET TO KNOW THEM BETTER.
BUT, BEFORE THAT, I'D LIKE TO PRESENT MR AND MRS DICKINSON.
THEY'RE THE THRILLED PARENTS OF THREE-MONTH-OLD MICHAEL DONOVAN DICKINSON, JR...
THE FIVE-HUNDREDTH BABY CONCEIVED THROUGH THE *PERFECT CHILD* PROGRAMME! OUR CONGRATULATIONS!!!
CLAP CLAP CLAP
15.

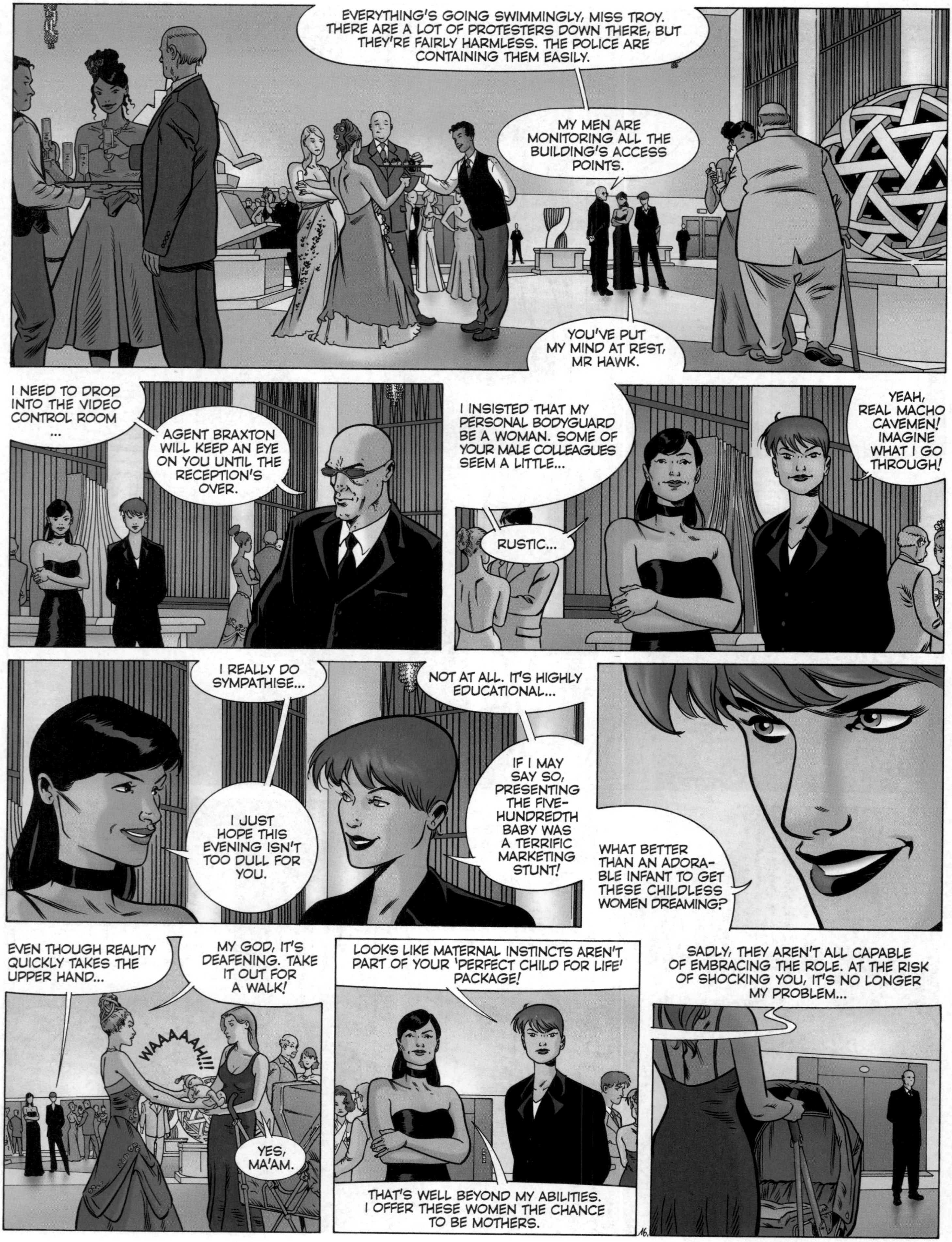
EVERYTHING'S GOING SWIMMINGLY, MISS TROY. THERE ARE A LOT OF PROTESTERS DOWN THERE, BUT THEY'RE FAIRLY HARMLESS. THE POLICE ARE CONTAINING THEM EASILY.
MY MEN ARE MONITORING ALL THE BUILDING'S ACCESS POINTS.
YOU'VE PUT MY MIND AT REST, MR HAWK.
I NEED TO DROP INTO THE VIDEO CONTROL ROOM ...
AGENT BRAXTON WILL KEEP AN EYE ON YOU UNTIL THE RECEPTION'S OVER.
I INSISTED THAT MY PERSONAL BODYGUARD BE A WOMAN. SOME OF YOUR MALE COLLEAGUES SEEM A LITTLE...
RUSTIC...
YEAH, REAL MACHO CAVEMEN! IMAGINE WHAT I GO THROUGH!
I REALLY DO SYMPATHISE...
I JUST HOPE THIS EVENING ISN'T TOO DULL FOR YOU.
NOT AT ALL. IT'S HIGHLY EDUCATIONAL...
IF I MAY SAY SO, PRESENTING THE FIVE-HUNDREDTH BABY WAS A TERRIFIC MARKETING STUNT!
WHAT BETTER THAN AN ADORABLE INFANT TO GET THESE CHILDLESS WOMEN DREAMING?
EVEN THOUGH REALITY QUICKLY TAKES THE UPPER HAND...
MY GOD, IT'S DEAFENING. TAKE IT OUT FOR A WALK!
WAAAAAH!!!
YES, MA'AM.
LOOKS LIKE MATERNAL INSTINCTS AREN'T PART OF YOUR 'PERFECT CHILD FOR LIFE' PACKAGE!
THAT'S WELL BEYOND MY ABILITIES. I OFFER THESE WOMEN THE CHANCE TO BE MOTHERS.
SADLY, THEY AREN'T ALL CAPABLE OF EMBRACING THE ROLE. AT THE RISK OF SHOCKING YOU, IT'S NO LONGER MY PROBLEM...

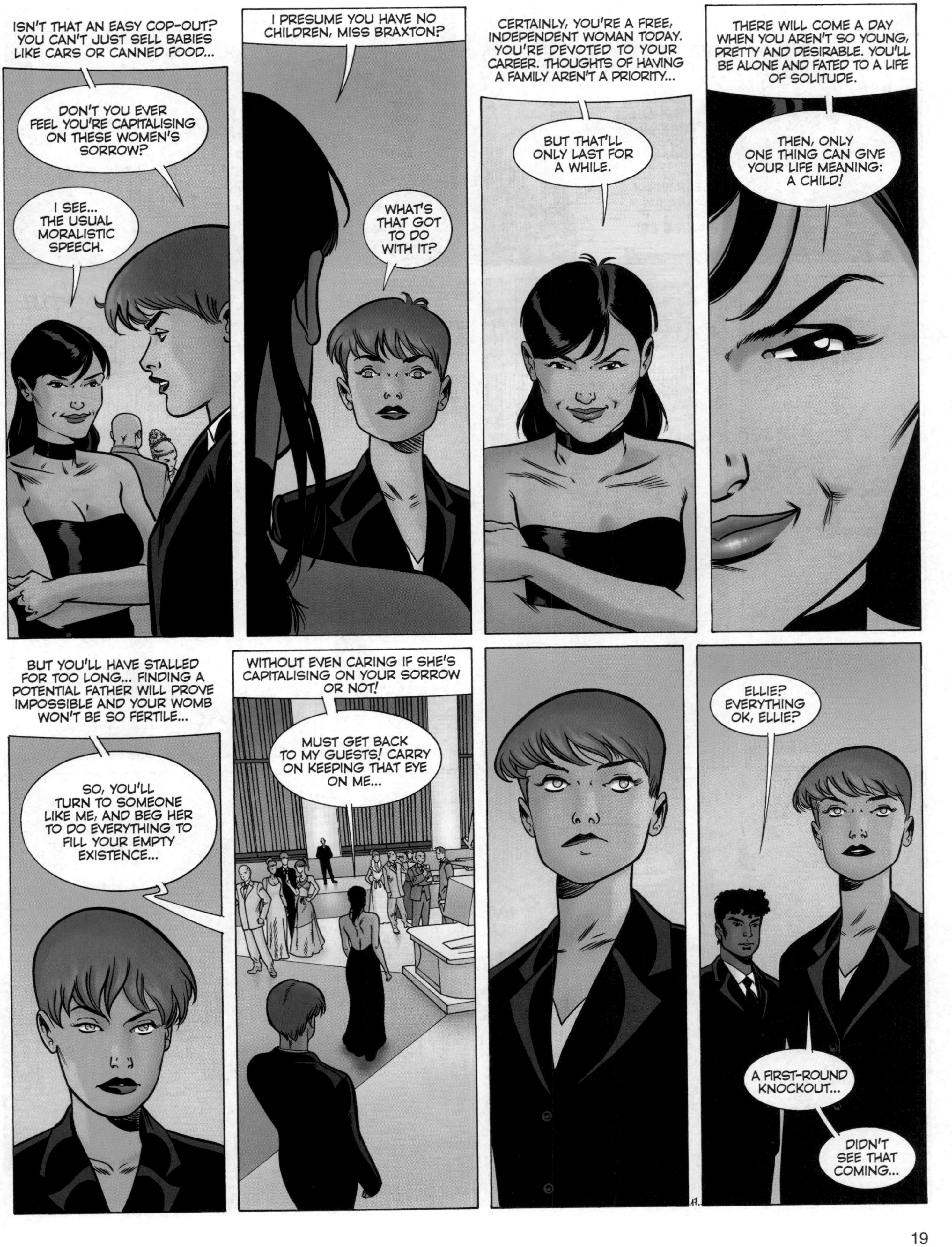

ISN'T THAT AN EASY COP-OUT? YOU CAN'T JUST SELL BABIES LIKE CARS OR CANNED FOOD...
DON'T YOU EVER FEEL YOU'RE CAPITALISING ON THESE WOMEN'S SORROW?
I SEE... THE USUAL MORALISTIC SPEECH.
I PRESUME YOU HAVE NO CHILDREN, MISS BRAXTON?
WHAT'S THAT GOT TO DO WITH IT?
CERTAINLY, YOU'RE A FREE, INDEPENDENT WOMAN TODAY. YOU'RE DEVOTED TO YOUR CAREER. THOUGHTS OF HAVING A FAMILY AREN'T A PRIORITY...
BUT THAT'LL ONLY LAST FOR A WHILE.
THERE WILL COME A DAY WHEN YOU AREN'T SO YOUNG, PRETTY AND DESIRABLE. YOU'LL BE ALONE AND FATED TO A LIFE OF SOLITUDE.
THEN, ONLY ONE THING CAN GIVE YOUR LIFE MEANING: A CHILD!
BUT YOU'LL HAVE STALLED FOR TOO LONG... FINDING A POTENTIAL FATHER WILL PROVE IMPOSSIBLE AND YOUR WOMB WON'T BE SO FERTILE...
SO, YOU'LL TURN TO SOMEONE LIKE ME, AND BEG HER TO DO EVERYTHING TO FILL YOUR EMPTY EXISTENCE...
WITHOUT EVEN CARING IF SHE'S CAPITALISING ON YOUR SORROW OR NOT!
MUST GET BACK TO MY GUESTS! CARRY ON KEEPING THAT EYE ON ME...
ELLIE? EVERYTHING OK, ELLIE?
A FIRST-ROUND KNOCKOUT...
DIDN'T SEE THAT COMING...

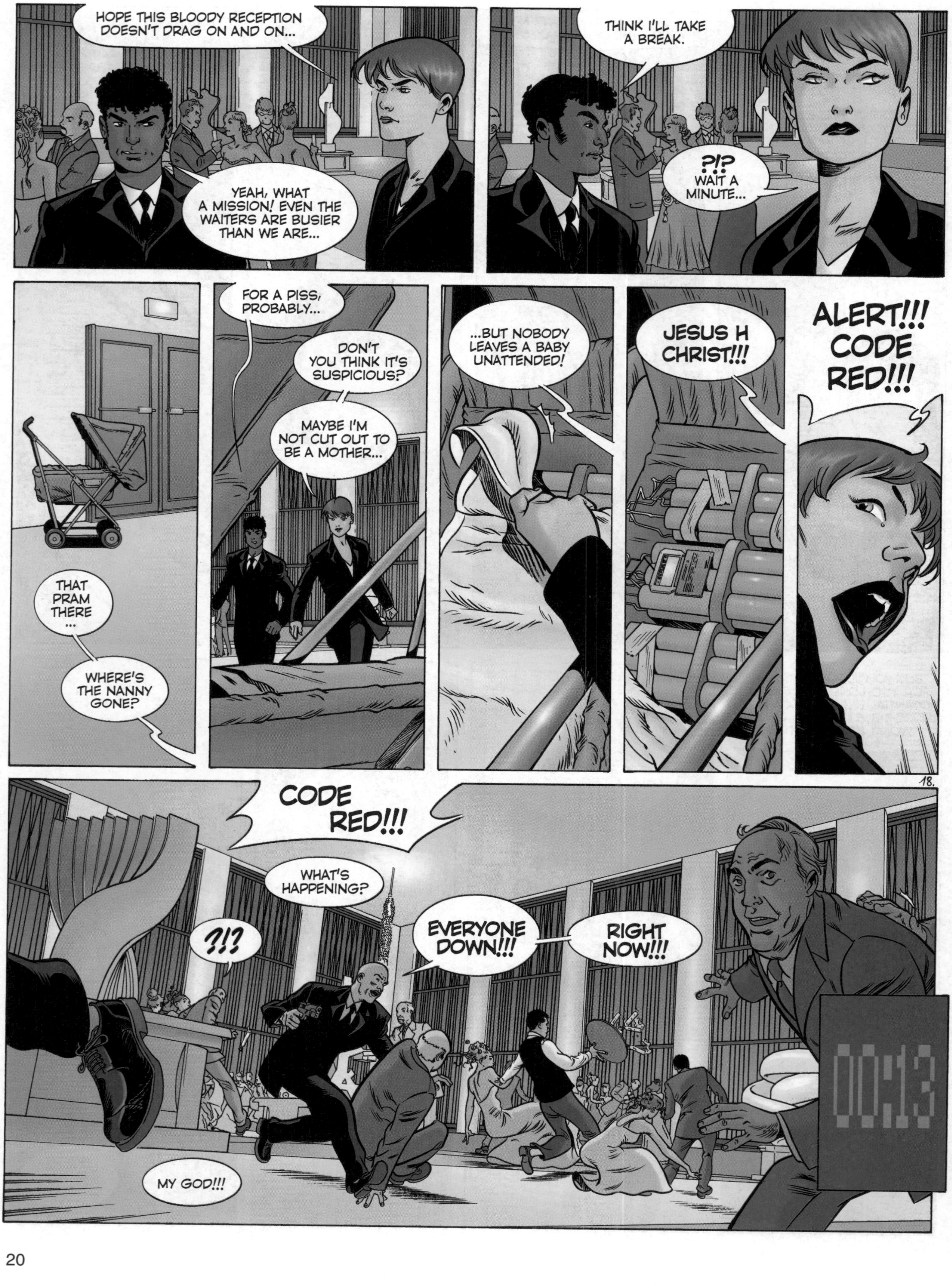
HOPE THIS BLOODY RECEPTION DOESN'T DRAG ON AND ON...
YEAH, WHAT A MISSION! EVEN THE WAITERS ARE BUSIER THAN WE ARE...
THINK I'LL TAKE A BREAK.
?!? WAIT A MINUTE...
THAT PRAM THERE ...
WHERE'S THE NANNY GONE?
FOR A PISS, PROBABLY...
DON'T YOU THINK IT'S SUSPICIOUS?
MAYBE I'M NOT CUT OUT TO BE A MOTHER...
...BUT NOBODY LEAVES A BABY UNATTENDED!
JESUS H CHRIST!!!
ALERT!!! CODE RED!!!
18.
CODE RED!!!
WHAT'S HAPPENING?
?!?
EVERYONE DOWN!!!
RIGHT NOW!!!
00:13
MY GOD!!!

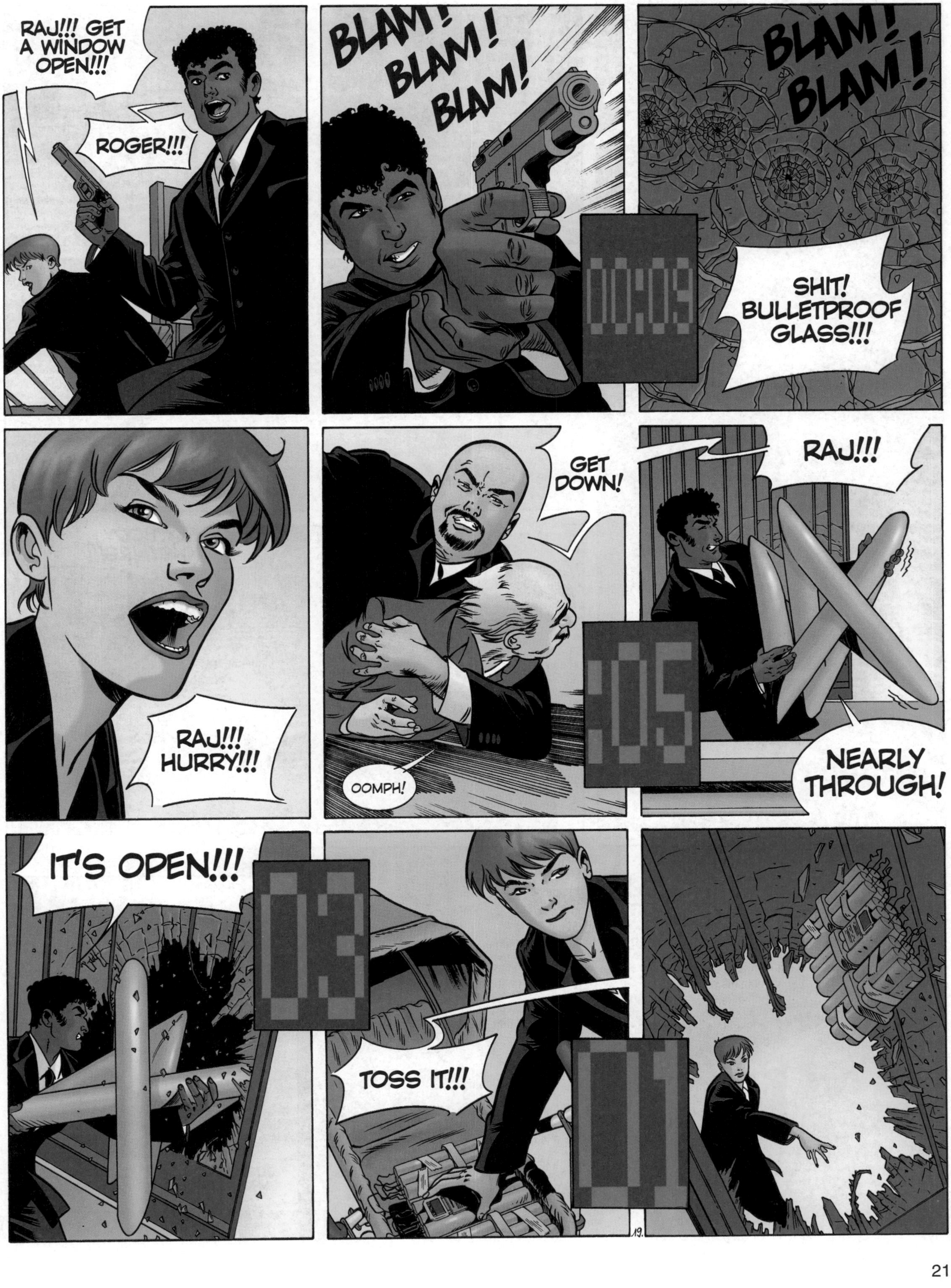
RAJ!!! GET A WINDOW OPEN!!!
ROGER!!!
BLAM! BLAM! BLAM!
00:09
BLAM! BLAM!
SHIT! BULLETPROOF GLASS!!!
RAJ!!! HURRY!!!
GET DOWN!
OOMPH!
:05
RAJ!!!
NEARLY THROUGH!
IT'S OPEN!!!
03
TOSS IT!!!
01
19.

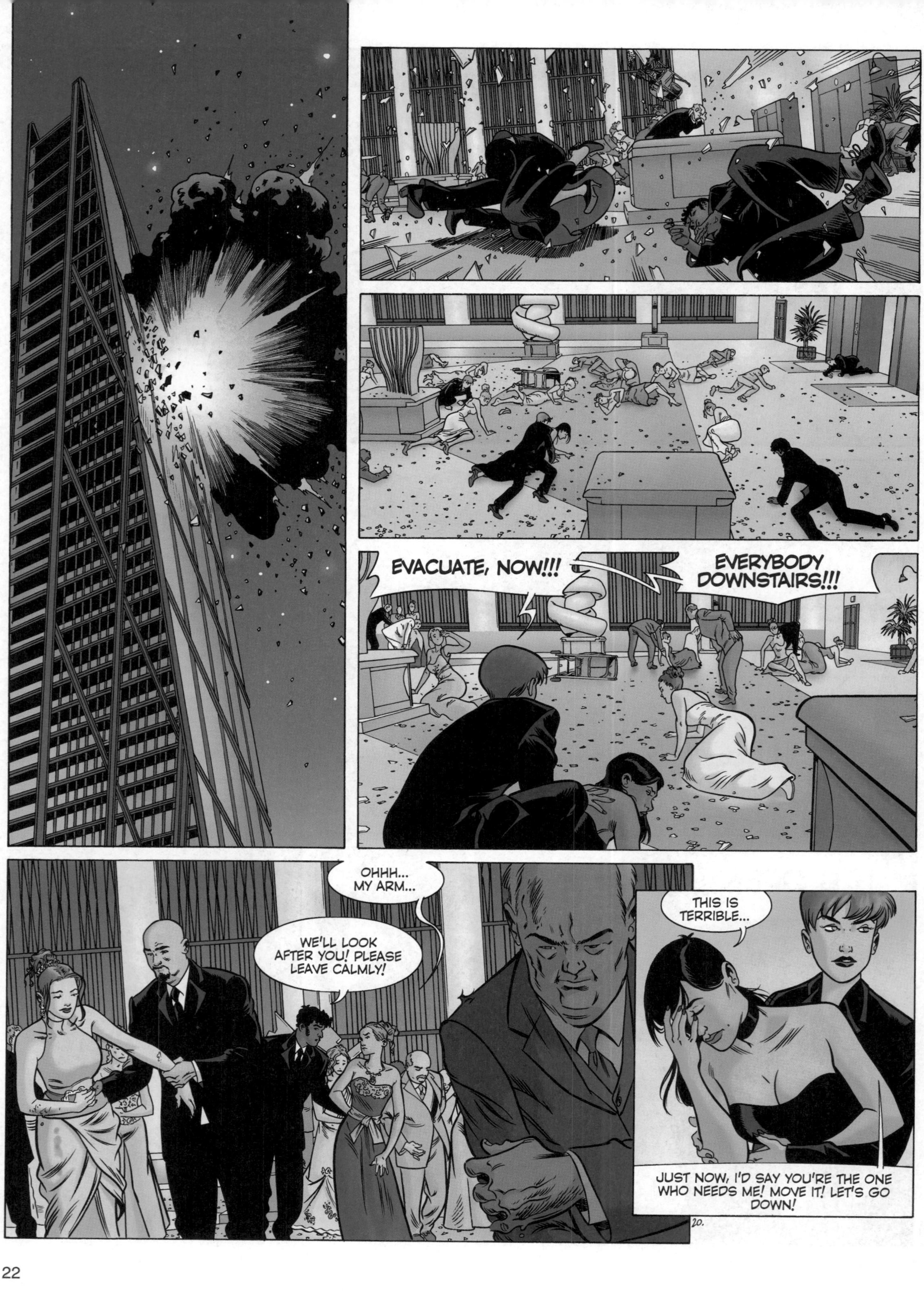
EVACUATE, NOW!!!
EVERYBODY DOWNSTAIRS!!!
OHHH... MY ARM...
WE'LL LOOK AFTER YOU! PLEASE LEAVE CALMLY!
THIS IS TERRIBLE...
JUST NOW, I'D SAY YOU'RE THE ONE WHO NEEDS ME! MOVE IT! LET'S GO DOWN!
20.

...LIVE FROM THE CRYSTAL BUILDING, WHOSE UPPER FLOORS WERE JUST ROCKED BY AN INTENSE BOMB BLAST.

IT TARGETED A *PERFECT CHILD* AGENCY RECEPTION BEING HELD AT THE TOP OF THE BUILDING. NO CASUALTIES ARE REPORTED.

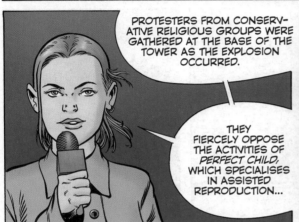

PROTESTERS FROM CONSERV- ATIVE RELIGIOUS GROUPS WERE GATHERED AT THE BASE OF THE TOWER AS THE EXPLOSION OCCURRED.

THEY FIERCELY OPPOSE THE ACTIVITIES OF *PERFECT CHILD*, WHICH SPECIALISES IN ASSISTED REPRODUCTION...

HERE WE SEE THE POLICE DETAINING SEVERAL INDIVIDUALS AMID THE GENERAL CONFUSION...

THE NEWS VULTURES ARE HAVING A FIELD DAY! A BOMB ATTACK, JESUS FREAKS...

PERFECT INGREDIENTS TO BUMP UP THE VIEWER RATINGS!

LUCKILY IT ALL ENDED WELL. EVEN DICKINSON, JR. GOT OUT UNSCATHED...

HE WAS FOUND BAWLING IN THE 12TH- FLOOR LADIES' TOILET, WHERE HIS 'NANNY' HAD DUMPED HIM. SHE HAD NO BEEF WITH HIM...

21.

SHE MANAGED TO EXIT THE BUILDING BEFORE THE COPS SHOWED UP.

QUESTION IS: WHO WAS SHE WORKING FOR?

FOR THESE BLOODY LOONIES? NAH, TOO OBVIOUS — THEY'RE IDEAL SCAPEGOATS...

SO WHO, THEN?

AGENT BRAXTON!

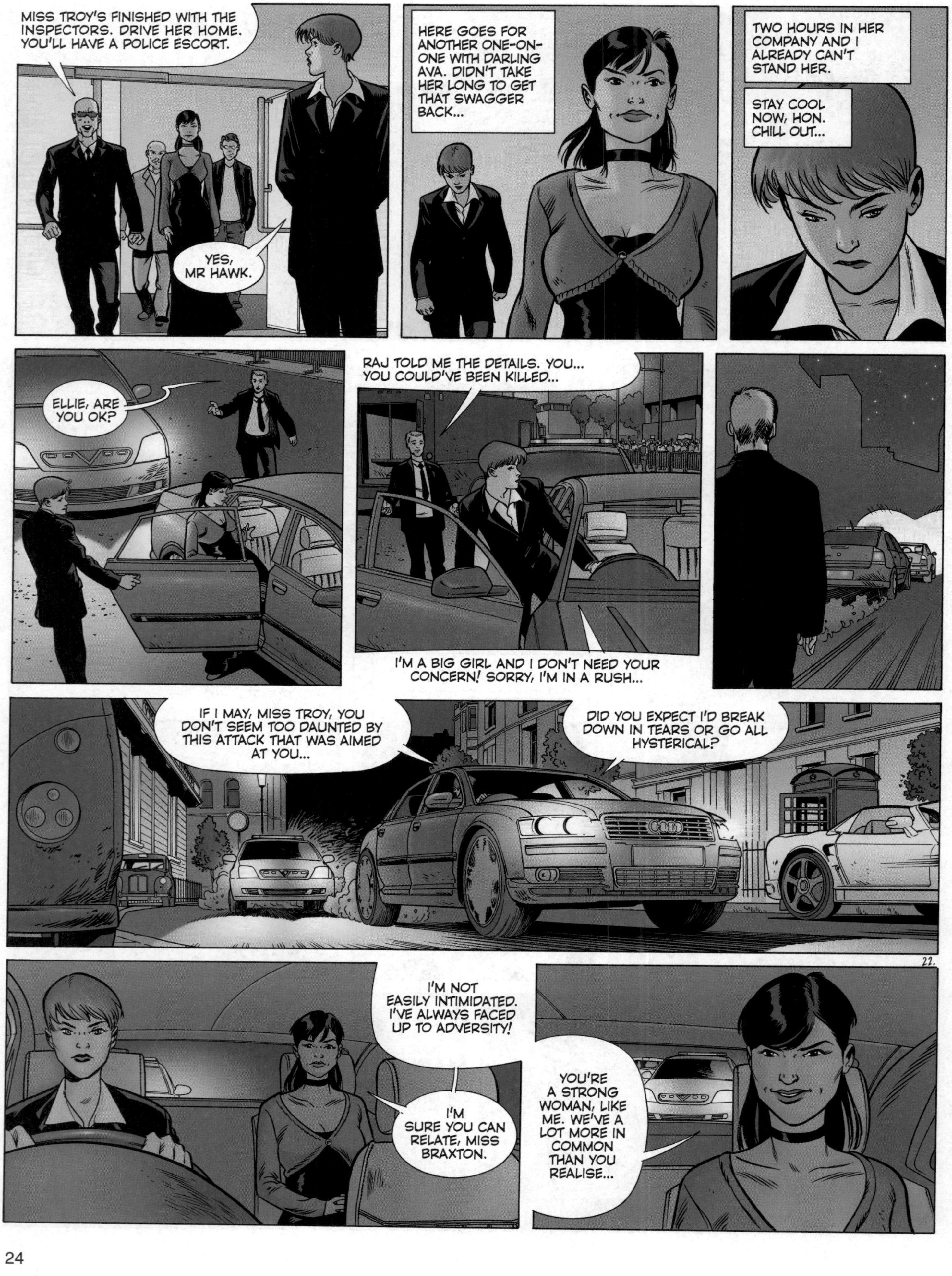
MISS TROY'S FINISHED WITH THE INSPECTORS. DRIVE HER HOME. YOU'LL HAVE A POLICE ESCORT.
YES, MR HAWK.
HERE GOES FOR ANOTHER ONE-ON-ONE WITH DARLING AVA. DIDN'T TAKE HER LONG TO GET THAT SWAGGER BACK...
TWO HOURS IN HER COMPANY AND I ALREADY CAN'T STAND HER.
STAY COOL NOW, HON. CHILL OUT...
ELLIE, ARE YOU OK?
RAJ TOLD ME THE DETAILS. YOU... YOU COULD'VE BEEN KILLED...
I'M A BIG GIRL AND I DON'T NEED YOUR CONCERN! SORRY, I'M IN A RUSH...
IF I MAY, MISS TROY, YOU DON'T SEEM TOO DAUNTED BY THIS ATTACK THAT WAS AIMED AT YOU...
DID YOU EXPECT I'D BREAK DOWN IN TEARS OR GO ALL HYSTERICAL?
I'M NOT EASILY INTIMIDATED. I'VE ALWAYS FACED UP TO ADVERSITY!
I'M SURE YOU CAN RELATE, MISS BRAXTON.
YOU'RE A STRONG WOMAN, LIKE ME. WE'VE A LOT MORE IN COMMON THAN YOU REALISE...
22.

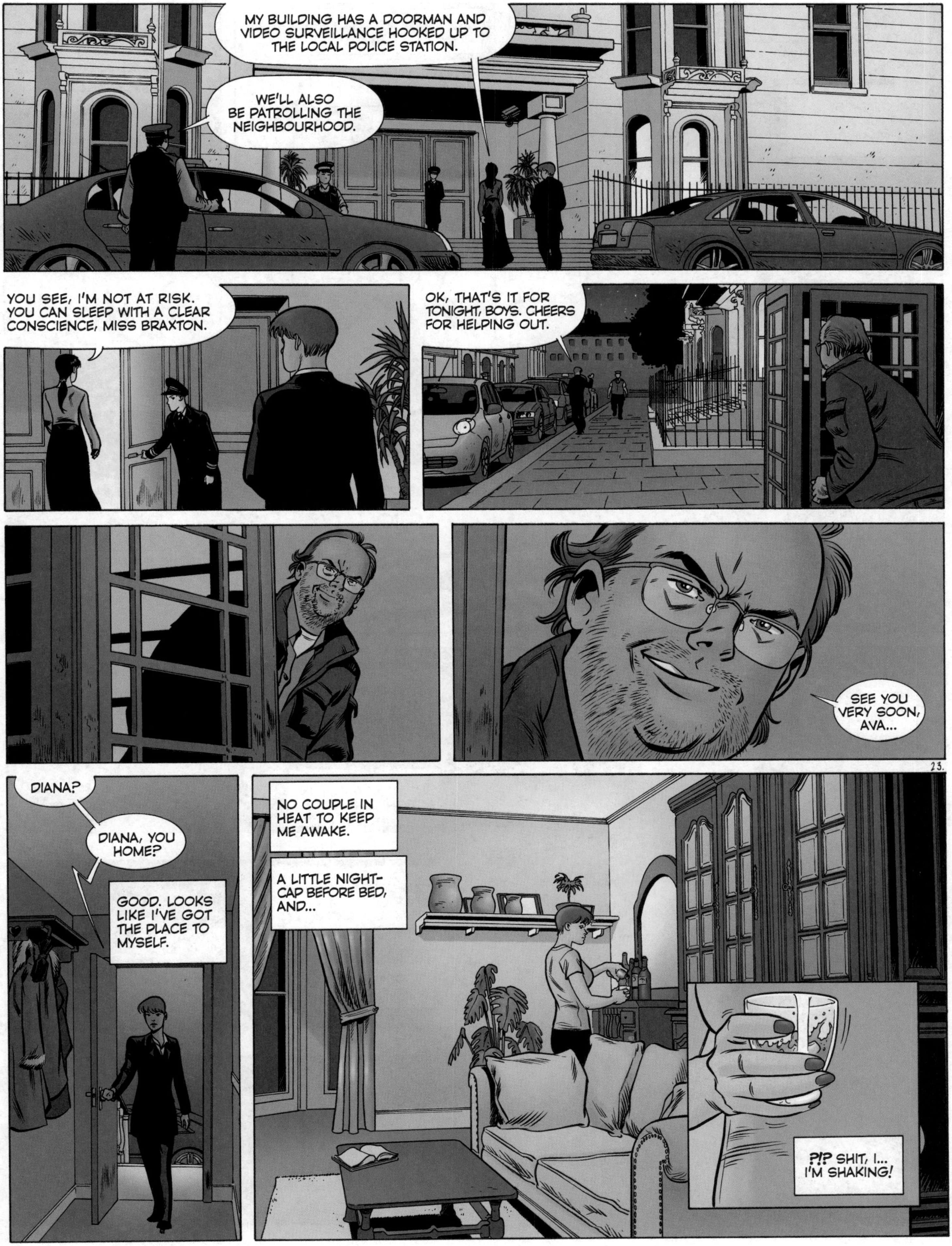
MY BUILDING HAS A DOORMAN AND VIDEO SURVEILLANCE HOOKED UP TO THE LOCAL POLICE STATION.
WE'LL ALSO BE PATROLLING THE NEIGHBOURHOOD.
YOU SEE, I'M NOT AT RISK. YOU CAN SLEEP WITH A CLEAR CONSCIENCE, MISS BRAXTON.
OK, THAT'S IT FOR TONIGHT, BOYS. CHEERS FOR HELPING OUT.
SEE YOU VERY SOON, AVA...
23.
DIANA?
DIANA, YOU HOME?
GOOD. LOOKS LIKE I'VE GOT THE PLACE TO MYSELF.
NO COUPLE IN HEAT TO KEEP ME AWAKE.
A LITTLE NIGHT-CAP BEFORE BED, AND...
?!? SHIT, I... I'M SHAKING!

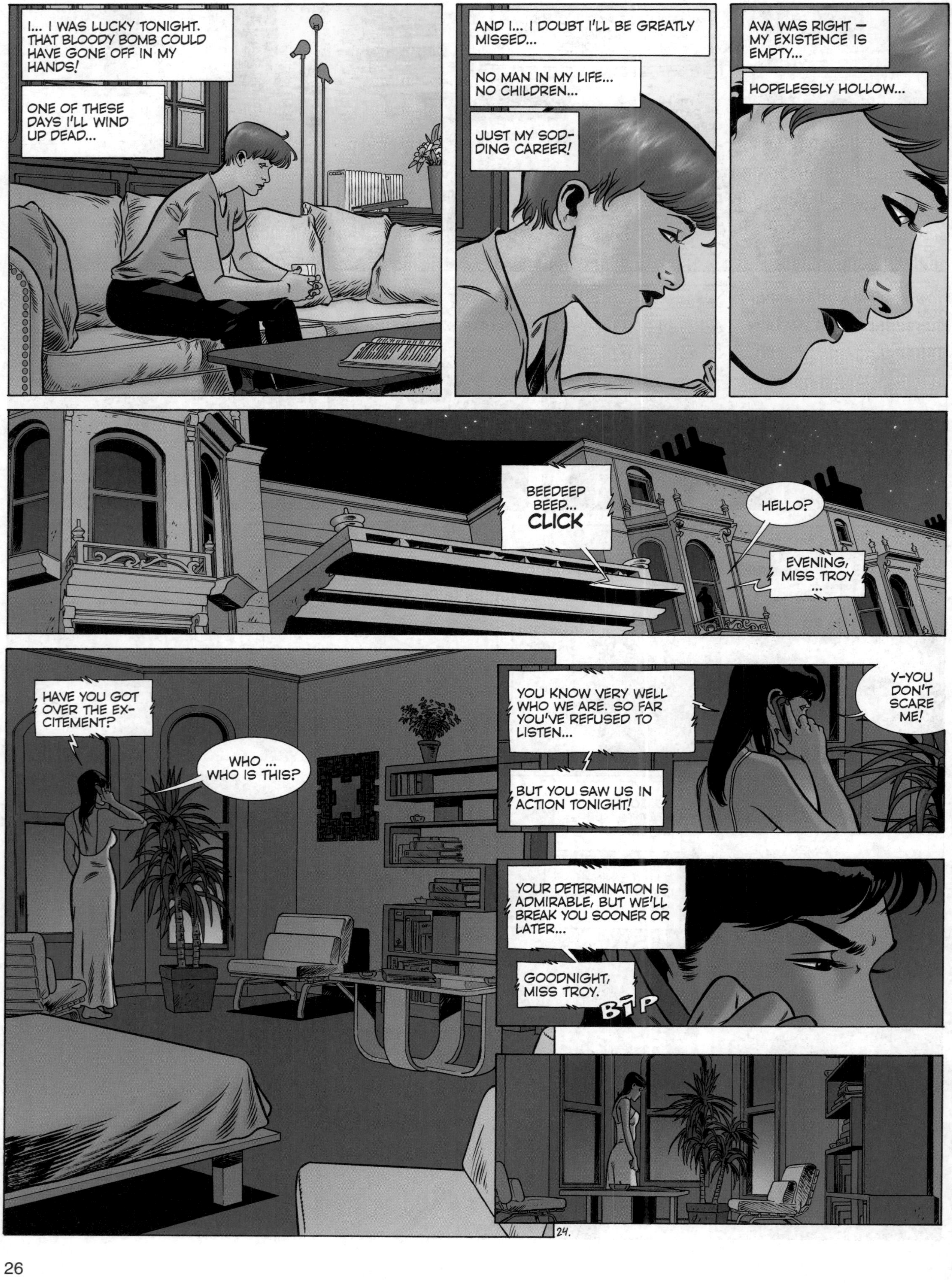
I... I WAS LUCKY TONIGHT. THAT BLOODY BOMB COULD HAVE GONE OFF IN MY HANDS!
ONE OF THESE DAYS I'LL WIND UP DEAD...
AND I... I DOUBT I'LL BE GREATLY MISSED...
NO MAN IN MY LIFE... NO CHILDREN...
JUST MY SOD-DING CAREER!
AVA WAS RIGHT — MY EXISTENCE IS EMPTY...
HOPELESSLY HOLLOW...
BEEDEEP BEEP... CLICK
HELLO?
EVENING, MISS TROY ...
HAVE YOU GOT OVER THE EX-CITEMENT?
WHO ... WHO IS THIS?
YOU KNOW VERY WELL WHO WE ARE. SO FAR YOU'VE REFUSED TO LISTEN...
BUT YOU SAW US IN ACTION TONIGHT!
Y-YOU DON'T SCARE ME!
YOUR DETERMINATION IS ADMIRABLE, BUT WE'LL BREAK YOU SOONER OR LATER...
GOODNIGHT, MISS TROY.
BIP
24.

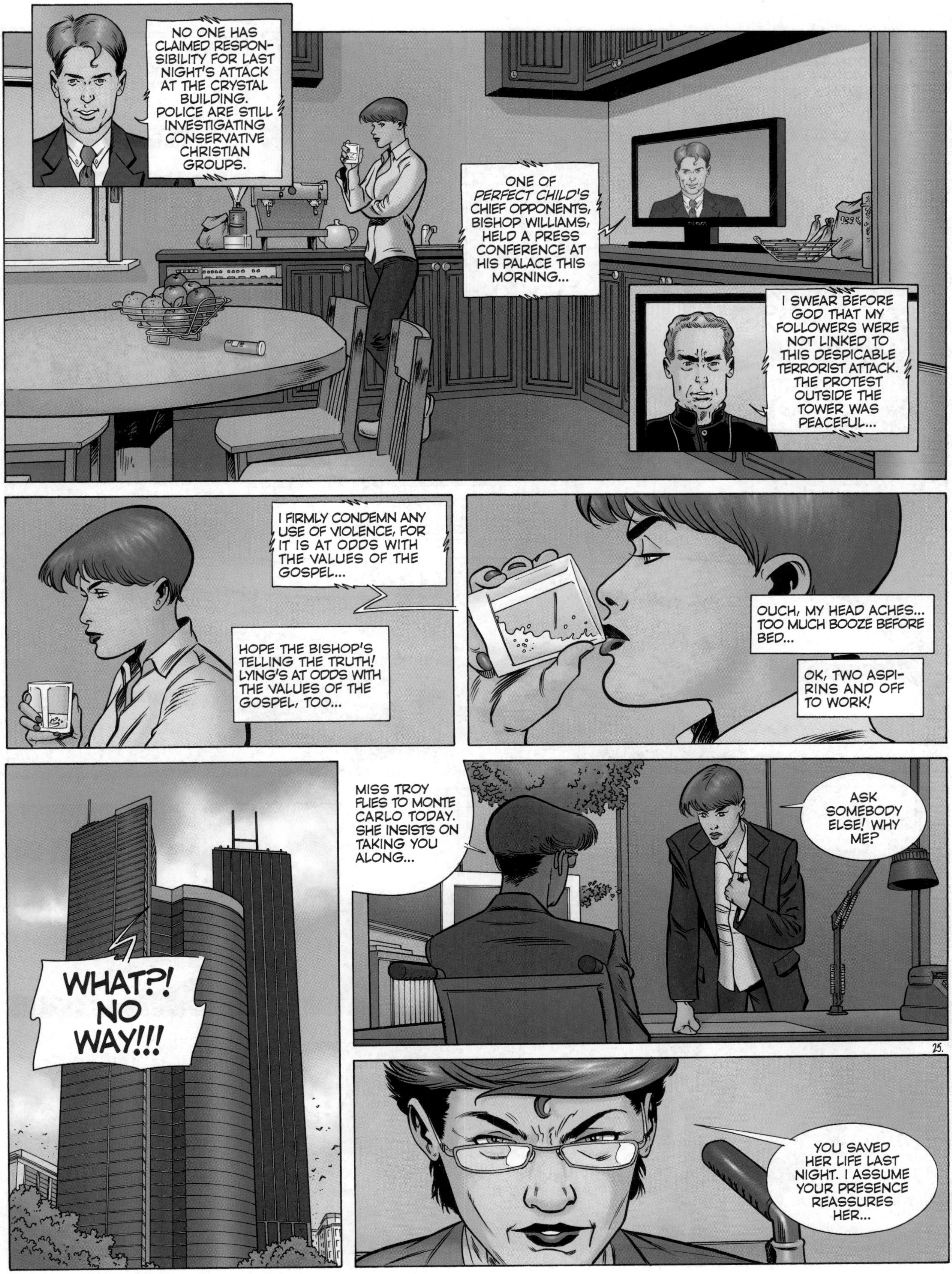
NO ONE HAS CLAIMED RESPONSIBILITY FOR LAST NIGHT'S ATTACK AT THE CRYSTAL BUILDING. POLICE ARE STILL INVESTIGATING CONSERVATIVE CHRISTIAN GROUPS.
ONE OF *PERFECT CHILD'S* CHIEF OPPONENTS, BISHOP WILLIAMS, HELD A PRESS CONFERENCE AT HIS PALACE THIS MORNING...
I SWEAR BEFORE GOD THAT MY FOLLOWERS WERE NOT LINKED TO THIS DESPICABLE TERRORIST ATTACK. THE PROTEST OUTSIDE THE TOWER WAS PEACEFUL...
I FIRMLY CONDEMN ANY USE OF VIOLENCE, FOR IT IS AT ODDS WITH THE VALUES OF THE GOSPEL...
HOPE THE BISHOP'S TELLING THE TRUTH! LYING'S AT ODDS WITH THE VALUES OF THE GOSPEL, TOO...
OUCH, MY HEAD ACHES... TOO MUCH BOOZE BEFORE BED...
OK, TWO ASPIRINS AND OFF TO WORK!
WHAT?! NO WAY!!!
MISS TROY FLIES TO MONTE CARLO TODAY. SHE INSISTS ON TAKING YOU ALONG...
ASK SOMEBODY ELSE! WHY ME?
25.
YOU SAVED HER LIFE LAST NIGHT. I ASSUME YOUR PRESENCE REASSURES HER...

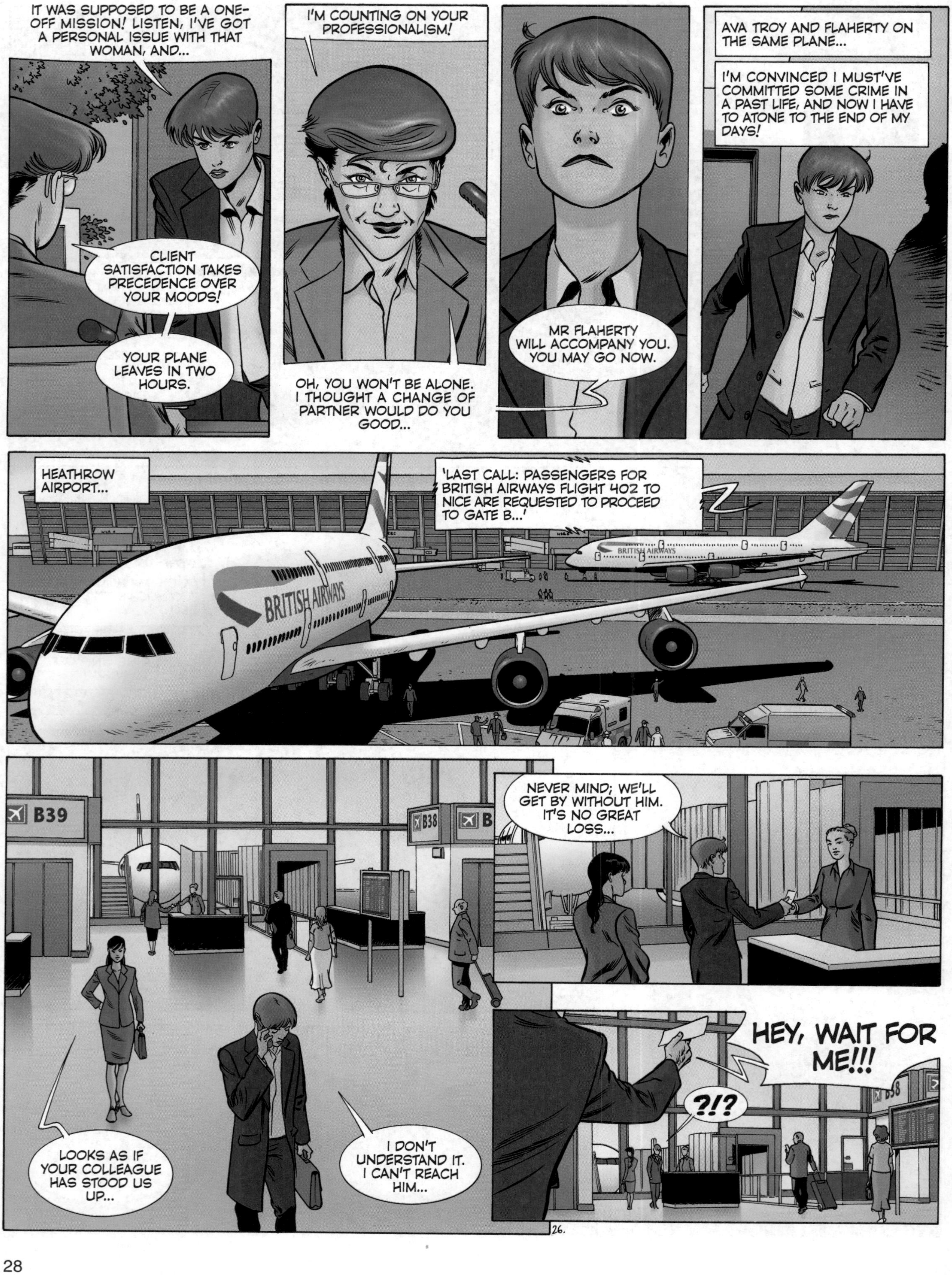
IT WAS SUPPOSED TO BE A ONE-OFF MISSION! LISTEN, I'VE GOT A PERSONAL ISSUE WITH THAT WOMAN, AND...
CLIENT SATISFACTION TAKES PRECEDENCE OVER YOUR MOODS!
YOUR PLANE LEAVES IN TWO HOURS.
I'M COUNTING ON YOUR PROFESSIONALISM!
OH, YOU WON'T BE ALONE. I THOUGHT A CHANGE OF PARTNER WOULD DO YOU GOOD...
MR FLAHERTY WILL ACCOMPANY YOU. YOU MAY GO NOW.
AVA TROY AND FLAHERTY ON THE SAME PLANE...
I'M CONVINCED I MUST'VE COMMITTED SOME CRIME IN A PAST LIFE, AND NOW I HAVE TO ATONE TO THE END OF MY DAYS!
HEATHROW AIRPORT...
'LAST CALL: PASSENGERS FOR BRITISH AIRWAYS FLIGHT 402 TO NICE ARE REQUESTED TO PROCEED TO GATE B...'
BRITISH AIRWAYS
BRITISH AIRWAYS
B39
B38
LOOKS AS IF YOUR COLLEAGUE HAS STOOD US UP...
I DON'T UNDERSTAND IT. I CAN'T REACH HIM...
NEVER MIND; WE'LL GET BY WITHOUT HIM. IT'S NO GREAT LOSS...
HEY, WAIT FOR ME!!!
?!?
B38
26.

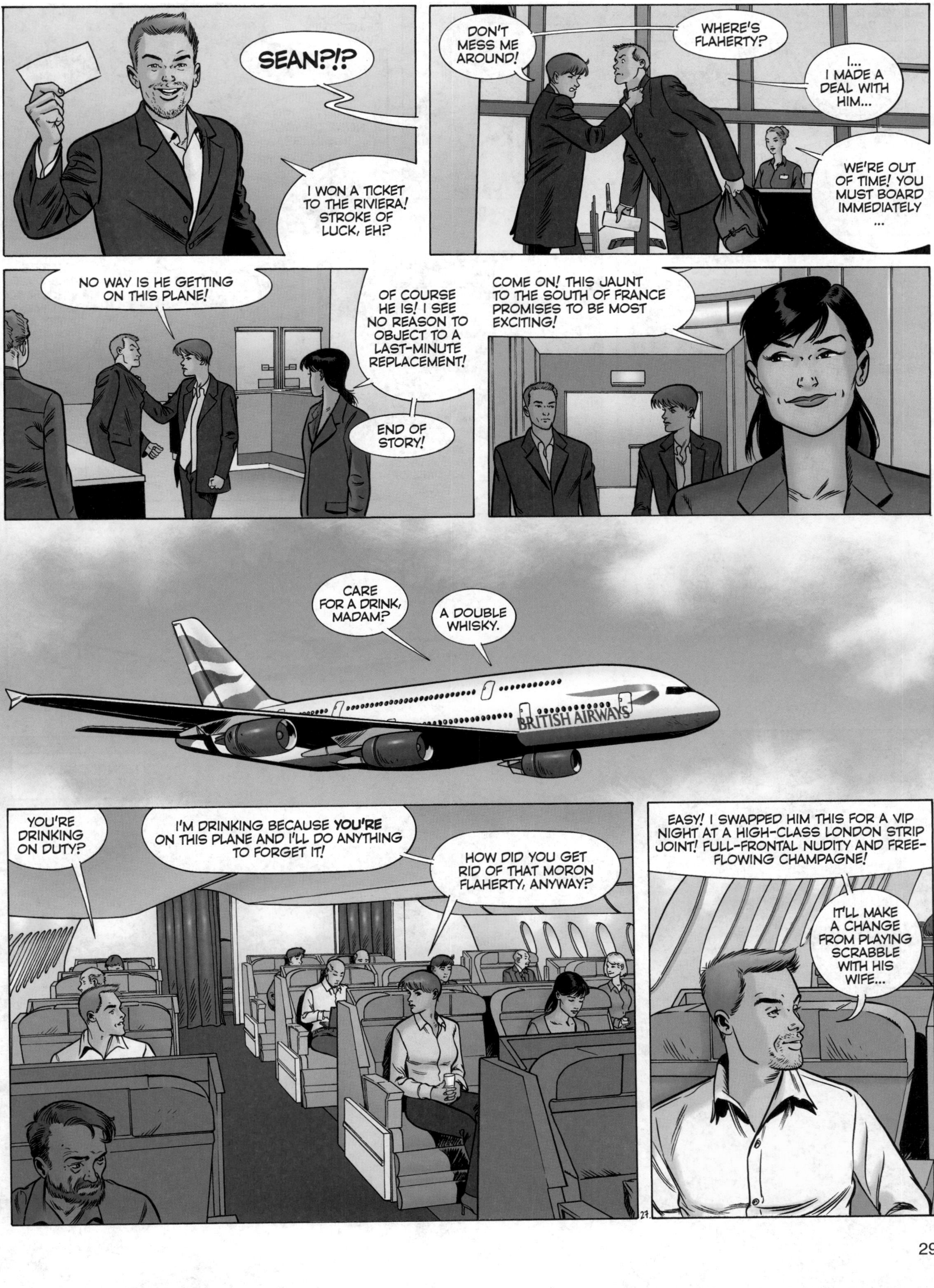
SEAN?!?
I WON A TICKET TO THE RIVIERA! STROKE OF LUCK, EH?
DON'T MESS ME AROUND!
WHERE'S FLAHERTY?
I... I MADE A DEAL WITH HIM...
WE'RE OUT OF TIME! YOU MUST BOARD IMMEDIATELY ...
NO WAY IS HE GETTING ON THIS PLANE!
OF COURSE HE IS! I SEE NO REASON TO OBJECT TO A LAST-MINUTE REPLACEMENT!
END OF STORY!
COME ON! THIS JAUNT TO THE SOUTH OF FRANCE PROMISES TO BE MOST EXCITING!
CARE FOR A DRINK, MADAM?
A DOUBLE WHISKY.
BRITISH AIRWAYS
YOU'RE DRINKING ON DUTY?
I'M DRINKING BECAUSE **YOU'RE** ON THIS PLANE AND I'LL DO ANYTHING TO FORGET IT!
HOW DID YOU GET RID OF THAT MORON FLAHERTY, ANYWAY?
EASY! I SWAPPED HIM THIS FOR A VIP NIGHT AT A HIGH-CLASS LONDON STRIP JOINT! FULL-FRONTAL NUDITY AND FREE-FLOWING CHAMPAGNE!
IT'LL MAKE A CHANGE FROM PLAYING SCRABBLE WITH HIS WIFE...

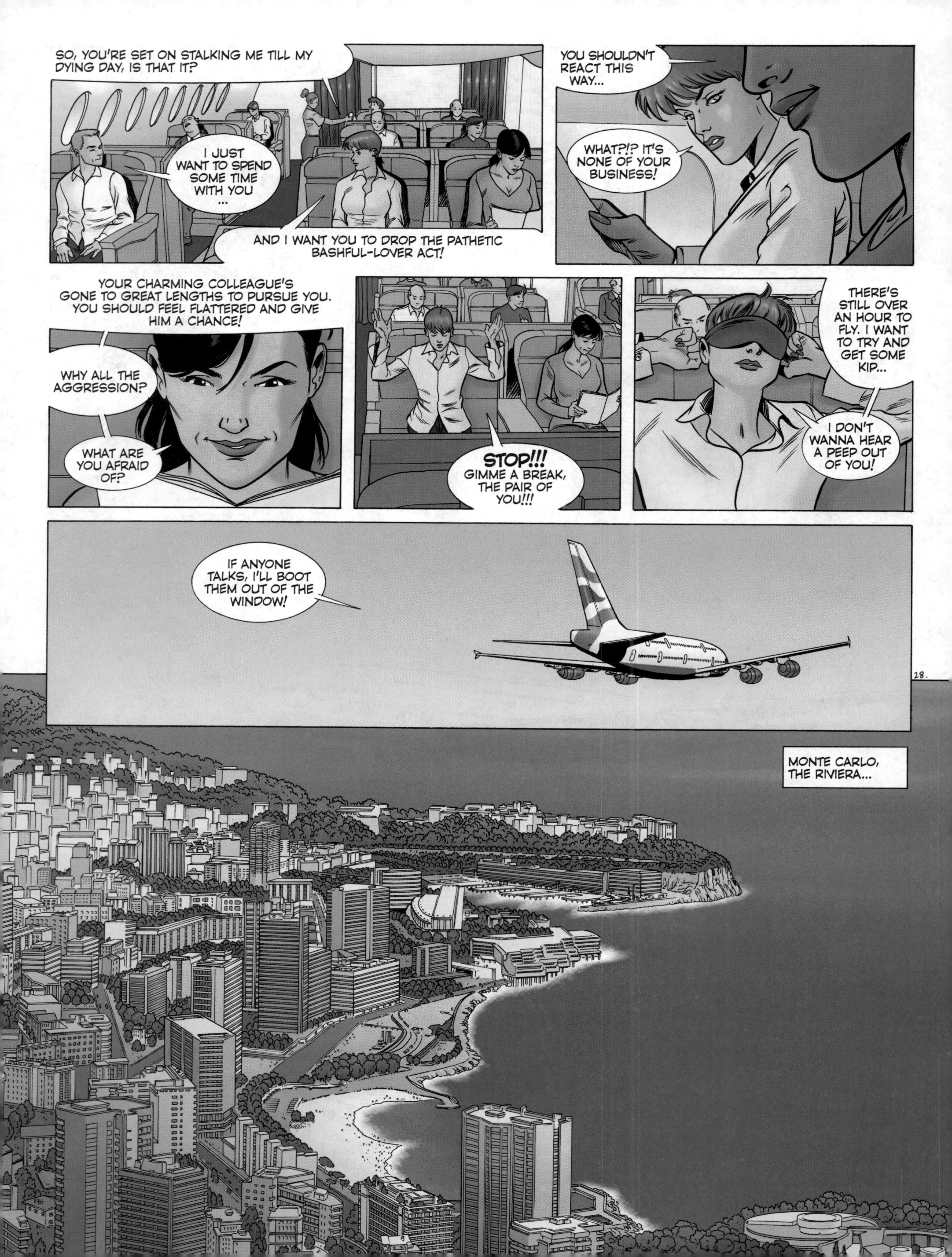
SO, YOU'RE SET ON STALKING ME TILL MY DYING DAY, IS THAT IT?
I JUST WANT TO SPEND SOME TIME WITH YOU ...
AND I WANT YOU TO DROP THE PATHETIC BASHFUL-LOVER ACT!
YOU SHOULDN'T REACT THIS WAY...
WHAT?!? IT'S NONE OF YOUR BUSINESS!
YOUR CHARMING COLLEAGUE'S GONE TO GREAT LENGTHS TO PURSUE YOU. YOU SHOULD FEEL FLATTERED AND GIVE HIM A CHANCE!
WHY ALL THE AGGRESSION?
WHAT ARE YOU AFRAID OF?
STOP!!! GIMME A BREAK, THE PAIR OF YOU!!!
THERE'S STILL OVER AN HOUR TO FLY. I WANT TO TRY AND GET SOME KIP...
I DON'T WANNA HEAR A PEEP OUT OF YOU!
IF ANYONE TALKS, I'LL BOOT THEM OUT OF THE WINDOW!
28.
MONTE CARLO, THE RIVIERA...

ALBERT II PRIVATE CLINIC, PRINCIPALITY OF MONACO...

MISS IVANOVIC HAS SUCCESSFULLY COMPLETED THE PROCEDURE.

THE OVARIAN STIMULATION PHASE JUST ENDED AFTER 15 DAYS OF INTENSIVE TREATMENT. THE LATEST ULTRASOUND SCANS SHOW HEALTHY FOLLICULAR DEVELOPMENT ...

SO WE DECIDED TO TRIGGER OVULATION ABOUT 12 HOURS AGO.

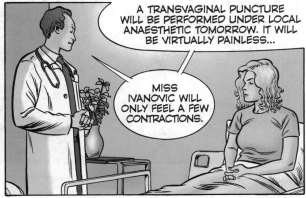

A TRANSVAGINAL PUNCTURE WILL BE PERFORMED UNDER LOCAL ANAESTHETIC TOMORROW. IT WILL BE VIRTUALLY PAINLESS...

MISS IVANOVIC WILL ONLY FEEL A FEW CONTRACTIONS.

THE OOCYTES WE RETRIEVE WILL BE FERTILISED IN OUR LABORATORY. THEN WE'LL CAREFULLY MONITOR THE DEVELOPMENT OF THE EMBRYOS.

NEXT, WE'LL MOVE ON TO THE CRUCIAL EMBRYO TRANSFER STAGE, WHICH CONCERNS YOU DIRECTLY, MRS DE BONNANCOURT.

ALLOW ME TO EXPLAIN THE DETAILS...

WHAT A RIVETING LECTURE! ALL SO COLD AND TECHNICAL...

HARD TO BELIEVE THEY'RE TALKING ABOUT CONCEIVING A CHILD. NO HINT OF EMOTION...

IT'S JUST A QUESTION OF CASH, AFTER ALL.

A WELL-OFF COUPLE LOOKING TO BUY A BABY, AS IF IT WERE A ROLLS-ROYCE...

A PRETTY YOUNG DONOR ENTICED BY THE EASY MONEY...

A DOCTOR WITH QUESTIONABLE ETHICS, WHO'LL TAKE A CUT OF THE COMMISSION...

NOT TO MENTION THE LOVELY AVA TROY, WHO'LL POCKET A NICE PROFIT WITH NO SCRUPLES WHATSOEVER...

WHAT A NIFTY LITTLE BUSINESS! NEXT, ALLOW NINE MONTHS FOR DELIVERY OF YOUR CUTE LITTLE HEIR...

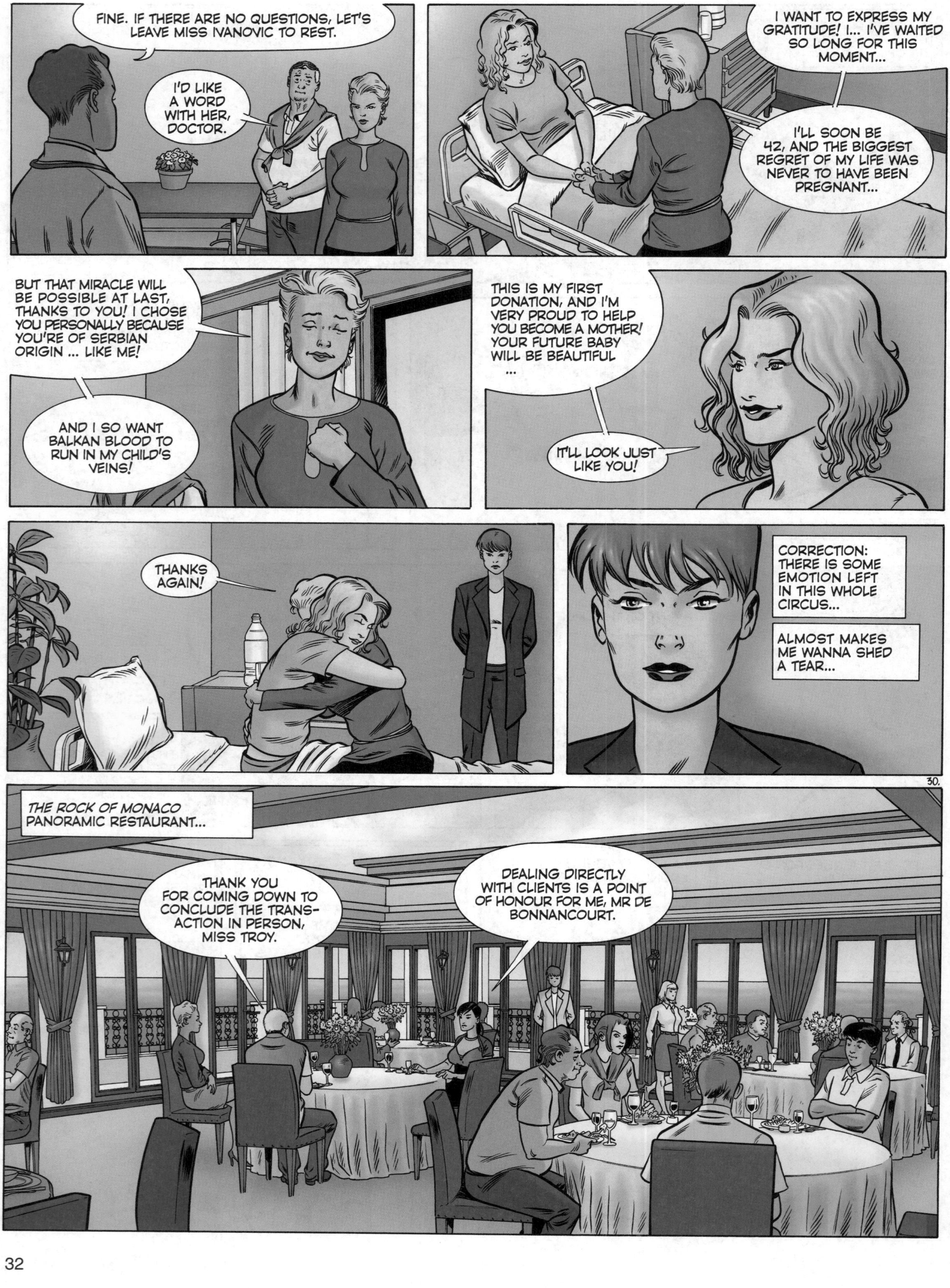
FINE. IF THERE ARE NO QUESTIONS, LET'S LEAVE MISS IVANOVIC TO REST.
I'D LIKE A WORD WITH HER, DOCTOR.
I WANT TO EXPRESS MY GRATITUDE! I... I'VE WAITED SO LONG FOR THIS MOMENT...
I'LL SOON BE 42, AND THE BIGGEST REGRET OF MY LIFE WAS NEVER TO HAVE BEEN PREGNANT...
BUT THAT MIRACLE WILL BE POSSIBLE AT LAST, THANKS TO YOU! I CHOSE YOU PERSONALLY BECAUSE YOU'RE OF SERBIAN ORIGIN ... LIKE ME!
AND I SO WANT BALKAN BLOOD TO RUN IN MY CHILD'S VEINS!
THIS IS MY FIRST DONATION, AND I'M VERY PROUD TO HELP YOU BECOME A MOTHER! YOUR FUTURE BABY WILL BE BEAUTIFUL ...
IT'LL LOOK JUST LIKE YOU!
THANKS AGAIN!
CORRECTION: THERE IS SOME EMOTION LEFT IN THIS WHOLE CIRCUS...
ALMOST MAKES ME WANNA SHED A TEAR...
30.
THE ROCK OF MONACO PANORAMIC RESTAURANT...
THANK YOU FOR COMING DOWN TO CONCLUDE THE TRANSACTION IN PERSON, MISS TROY.
DEALING DIRECTLY WITH CLIENTS IS A POINT OF HONOUR FOR ME, MR DE BONNANCOURT.

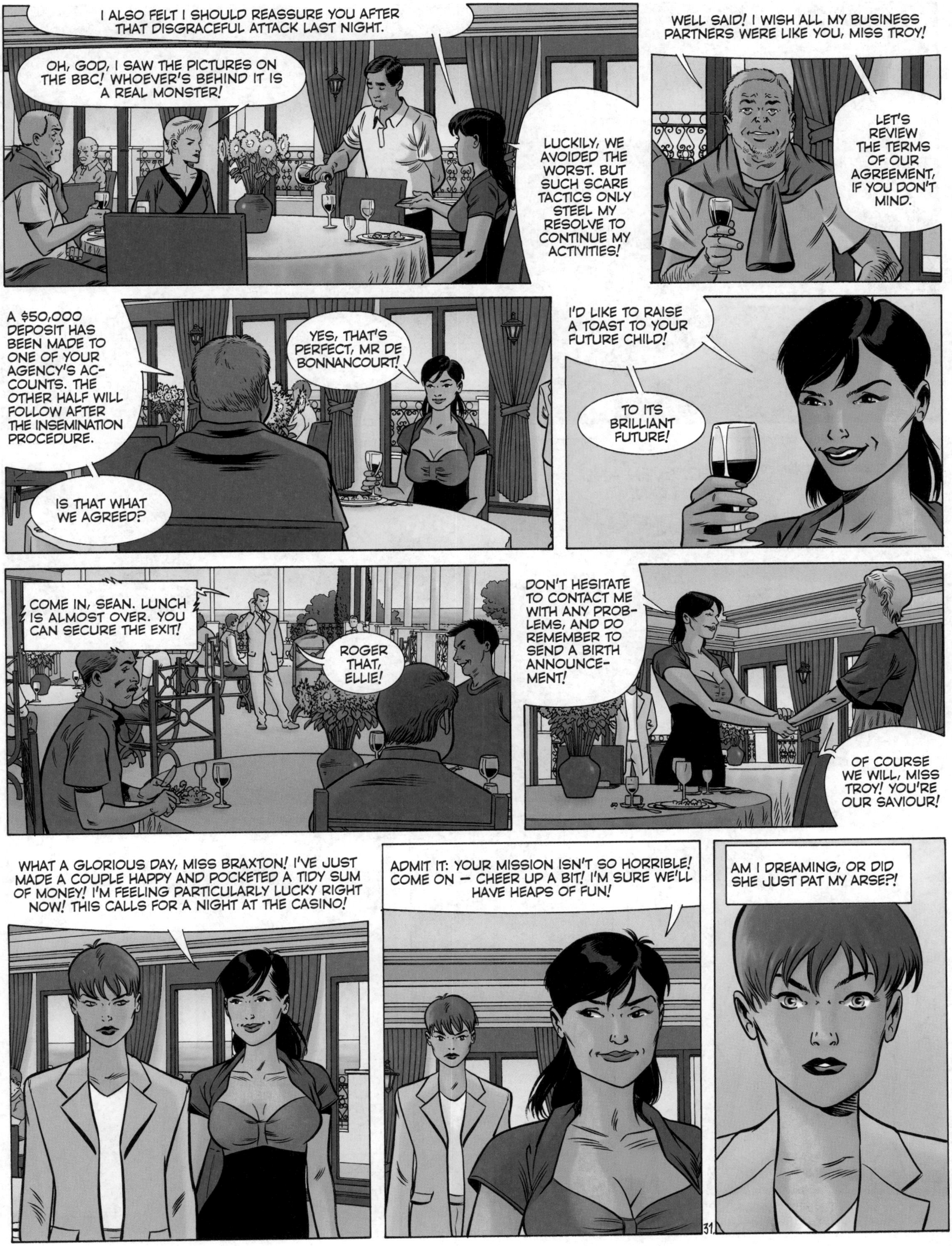
I ALSO FELT I SHOULD REASSURE YOU AFTER THAT DISGRACEFUL ATTACK LAST NIGHT.
OH, GOD, I SAW THE PICTURES ON THE BBC! WHOEVER'S BEHIND IT IS A REAL MONSTER!
LUCKILY, WE AVOIDED THE WORST. BUT SUCH SCARE TACTICS ONLY STEEL MY RESOLVE TO CONTINUE MY ACTIVITIES!
WELL SAID! I WISH ALL MY BUSINESS PARTNERS WERE LIKE YOU, MISS TROY!
LET'S REVIEW THE TERMS OF OUR AGREEMENT, IF YOU DON'T MIND.
A $50,000 DEPOSIT HAS BEEN MADE TO ONE OF YOUR AGENCY'S AC-COUNTS. THE OTHER HALF WILL FOLLOW AFTER THE INSEMINATION PROCEDURE.
IS THAT WHAT WE AGREED?
YES, THAT'S PERFECT, MR DE BONNANCOURT!
I'D LIKE TO RAISE A TOAST TO YOUR FUTURE CHILD!
TO ITS BRILLIANT FUTURE!
COME IN, SEAN. LUNCH IS ALMOST OVER. YOU CAN SECURE THE EXIT!
ROGER THAT, ELLIE!
DON'T HESITATE TO CONTACT ME WITH ANY PROB-LEMS, AND DO REMEMBER TO SEND A BIRTH ANNOUNCE-MENT!
OF COURSE WE WILL, MISS TROY! YOU'RE OUR SAVIOUR!
WHAT A GLORIOUS DAY, MISS BRAXTON! I'VE JUST MADE A COUPLE HAPPY AND POCKETED A TIDY SUM OF MONEY! I'M FEELING PARTICULARLY LUCKY RIGHT NOW! THIS CALLS FOR A NIGHT AT THE CASINO!
ADMIT IT: YOUR MISSION ISN'T SO HORRIBLE! COME ON — CHEER UP A BIT! I'M SURE WE'LL HAVE HEAPS OF FUN!
AM I DREAMING, OR DID SHE JUST PAT MY ARSE?!
31

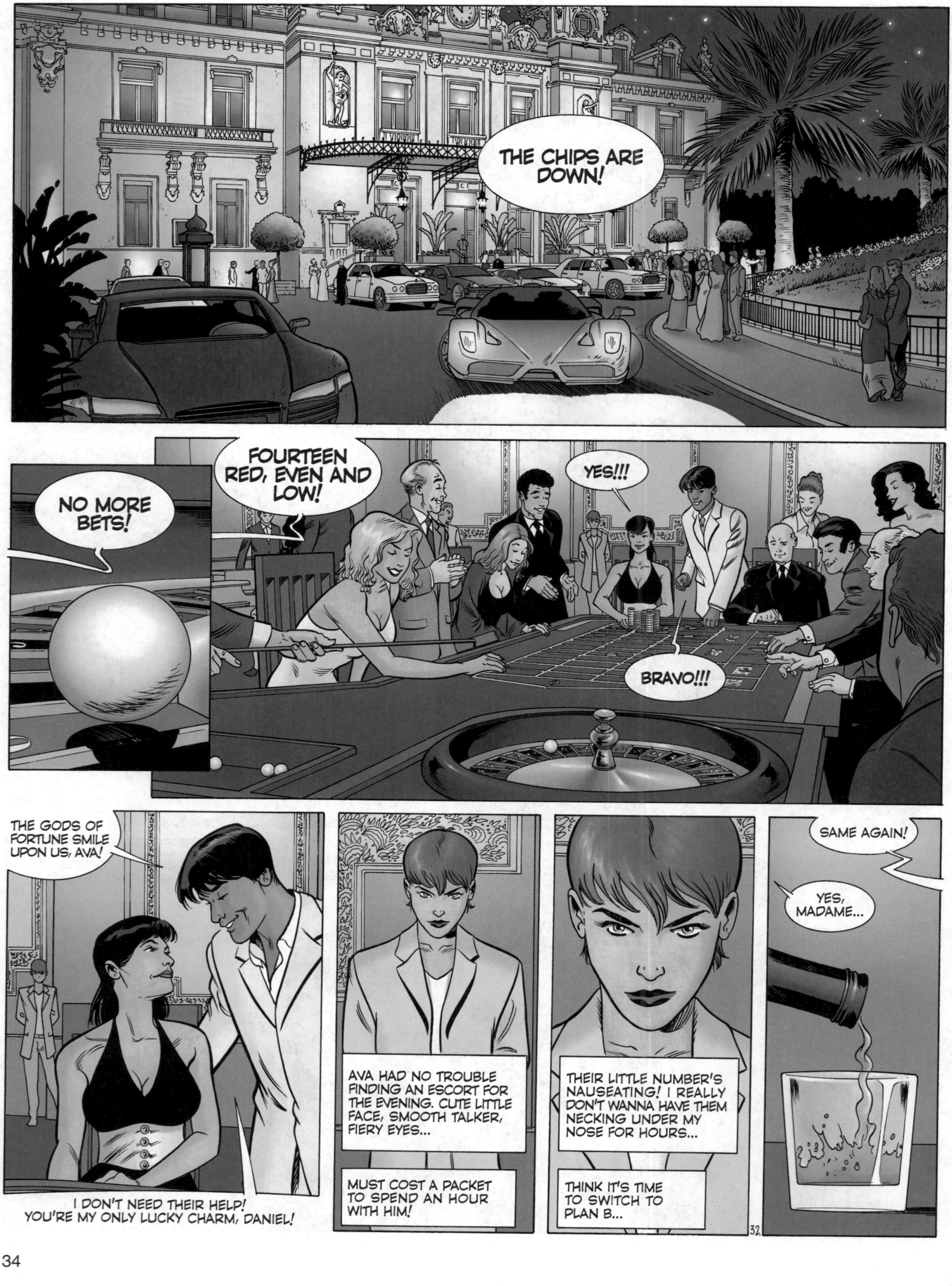
THE CHIPS ARE DOWN!
NO MORE BETS!
FOURTEEN RED, EVEN AND LOW!
YES!!!
BRAVO!!!
THE GODS OF FORTUNE SMILE UPON US, AVA!
I DON'T NEED THEIR HELP! YOU'RE MY ONLY LUCKY CHARM, DANIEL!
AVA HAD NO TROUBLE FINDING AN ESCORT FOR THE EVENING. CUTE LITTLE FACE, SMOOTH TALKER, FIERY EYES...
MUST COST A PACKET TO SPEND AN HOUR WITH HIM!
THEIR LITTLE NUMBER'S NAUSEATING! I REALLY DON'T WANNA HAVE THEM NECKING UNDER MY NOSE FOR HOURS...
THINK IT'S TIME TO SWITCH TO PLAN B...
SAME AGAIN!
YES, MADAME...

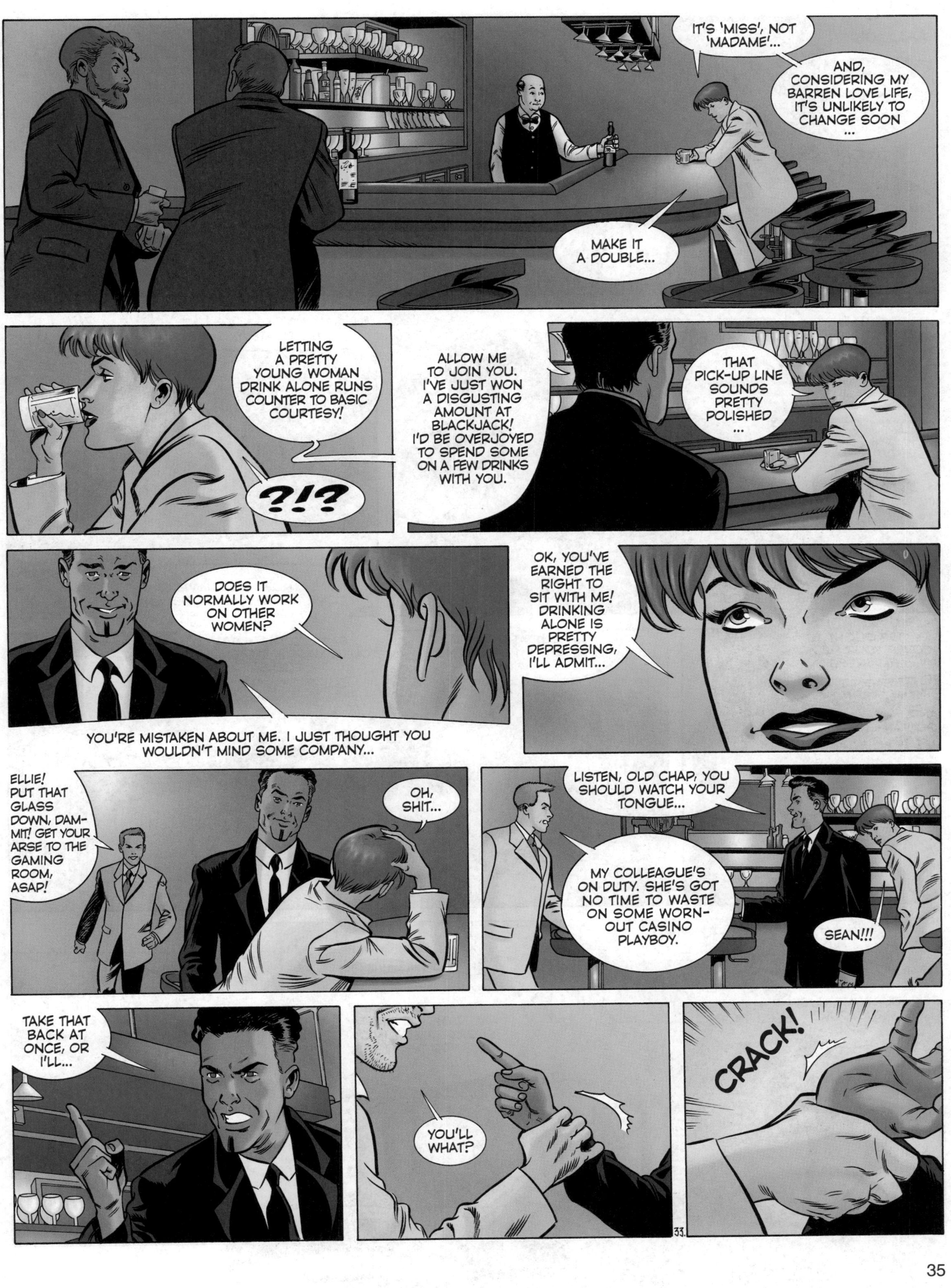
IT'S 'MISS', NOT 'MADAME'...
AND, CONSIDERING MY BARREN LOVE LIFE, IT'S UNLIKELY TO CHANGE SOON ...
MAKE IT A DOUBLE...
LETTING A PRETTY YOUNG WOMAN DRINK ALONE RUNS COUNTER TO BASIC COURTESY!
?!?
ALLOW ME TO JOIN YOU. I'VE JUST WON A DISGUSTING AMOUNT AT BLACKJACK! I'D BE OVERJOYED TO SPEND SOME ON A FEW DRINKS WITH YOU.
THAT PICK-UP LINE SOUNDS PRETTY POLISHED ...
DOES IT NORMALLY WORK ON OTHER WOMEN?
YOU'RE MISTAKEN ABOUT ME. I JUST THOUGHT YOU WOULDN'T MIND SOME COMPANY...
OK, YOU'VE EARNED THE RIGHT TO SIT WITH ME! DRINKING ALONE IS PRETTY DEPRESSING, I'LL ADMIT...
ELLIE! PUT THAT GLASS DOWN, DAM-MIT! GET YOUR ARSE TO THE GAMING ROOM, ASAP!
OH, SHIT...
LISTEN, OLD CHAP, YOU SHOULD WATCH YOUR TONGUE...
MY COLLEAGUE'S ON DUTY. SHE'S GOT NO TIME TO WASTE ON SOME WORN-OUT CASINO PLAYBOY.
SEAN!!!
TAKE THAT BACK AT ONCE, OR I'LL...
YOU'LL WHAT?
CRACK!
33.

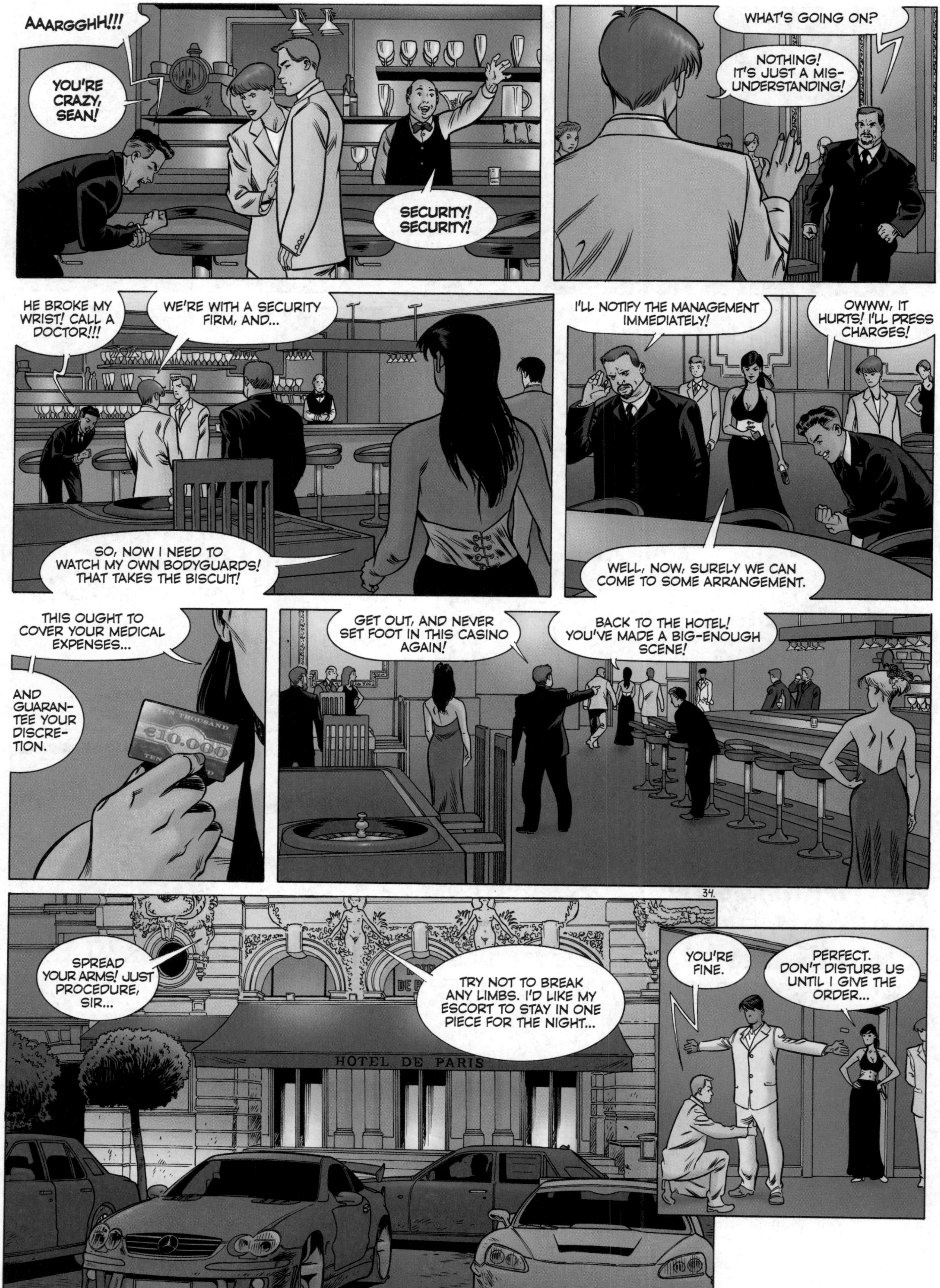
AAARGGHH!!!
YOU'RE CRAZY, SEAN!
SECURITY! SECURITY!
WHAT'S GOING ON?
NOTHING! IT'S JUST A MIS-UNDERSTANDING!
HE BROKE MY WRIST! CALL A DOCTOR!!!
WE'RE WITH A SECURITY FIRM, AND...
SO, NOW I NEED TO WATCH MY OWN BODYGUARDS! THAT TAKES THE BISCUIT!
I'LL NOTIFY THE MANAGEMENT IMMEDIATELY!
OWWW, IT HURTS! I'LL PRESS CHARGES!
WELL, NOW, SURELY WE CAN COME TO SOME ARRANGEMENT.
THIS OUGHT TO COVER YOUR MEDICAL EXPENSES...
AND GUARAN-TEE YOUR DISCRE-TION.
TEN THOUSAND
€10.000
GET OUT, AND NEVER SET FOOT IN THIS CASINO AGAIN!
BACK TO THE HOTEL! YOU'VE MADE A BIG-ENOUGH SCENE!
34.
SPREAD YOUR ARMS! JUST PROCEDURE, SIR...
TRY NOT TO BREAK ANY LIMBS. I'D LIKE MY ESCORT TO STAY IN ONE PIECE FOR THE NIGHT...
HOTEL DE PARIS
YOU'RE FINE.
PERFECT. DON'T DISTURB US UNTIL I GIVE THE ORDER...

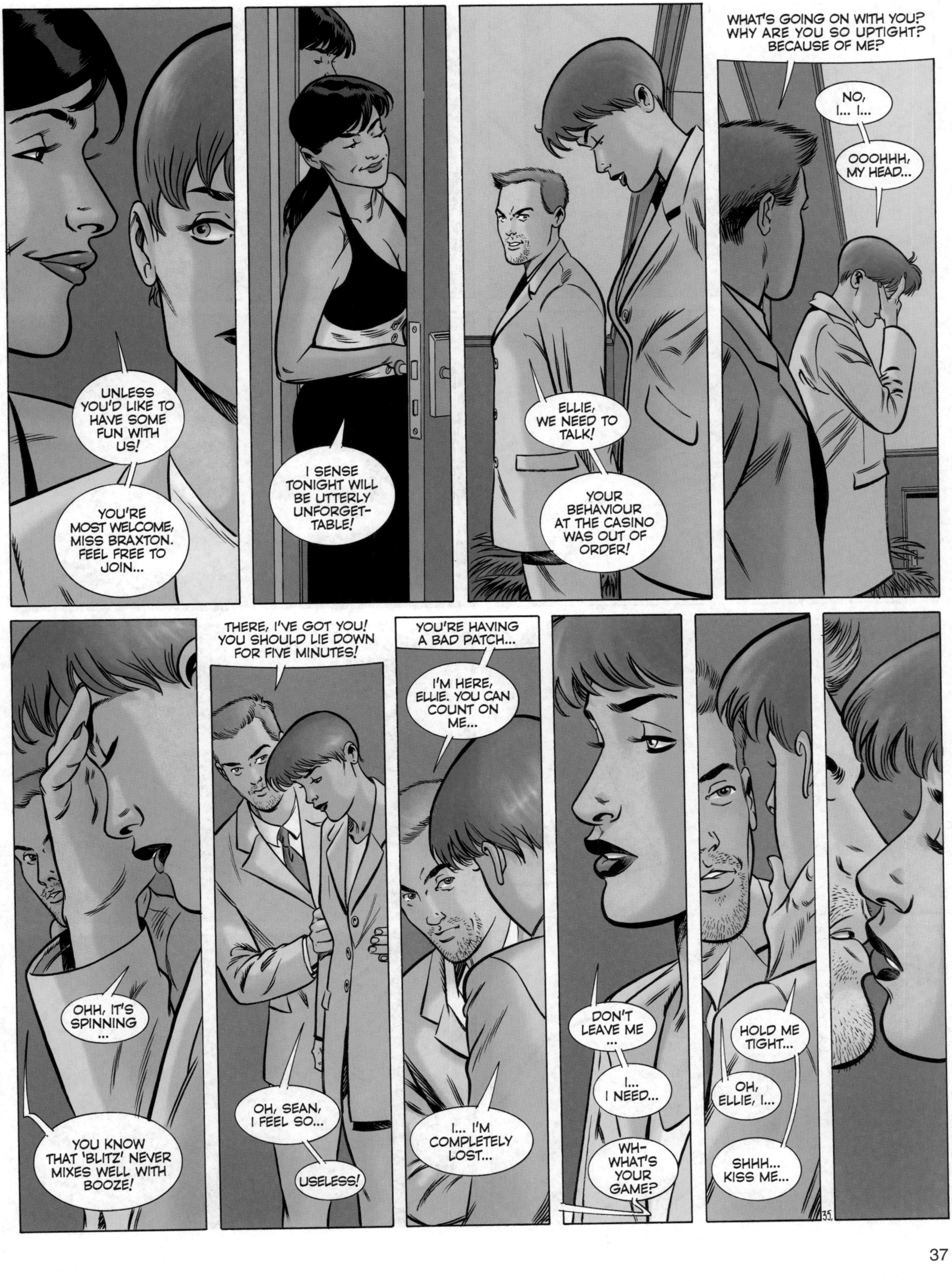
UNLESS YOU'D LIKE TO HAVE SOME FUN WITH US!
YOU'RE MOST WELCOME, MISS BRAXTON. FEEL FREE TO JOIN...
I SENSE TONIGHT WILL BE UTTERLY UNFORGET-TABLE!
ELLIE, WE NEED TO TALK!
YOUR BEHAVIOUR AT THE CASINO WAS OUT OF ORDER!
WHAT'S GOING ON WITH YOU? WHY ARE YOU SO UPTIGHT? BECAUSE OF ME?
NO, I... I...
OOOHHH, MY HEAD...
OHH, IT'S SPINNING ...
YOU KNOW THAT 'BLITZ' NEVER MIXES WELL WITH BOOZE!
THERE, I'VE GOT YOU! YOU SHOULD LIE DOWN FOR FIVE MINUTES!
OH, SEAN, I FEEL SO...
USELESS!
YOU'RE HAVING A BAD PATCH...
I'M HERE, ELLIE. YOU CAN COUNT ON ME...
I... I'M COMPLETELY LOST...
DON'T LEAVE ME ...
I... I NEED...
WH-WHAT'S YOUR GAME?
HOLD ME TIGHT...
OH, ELLIE, I...
SHHH... KISS ME...
35.

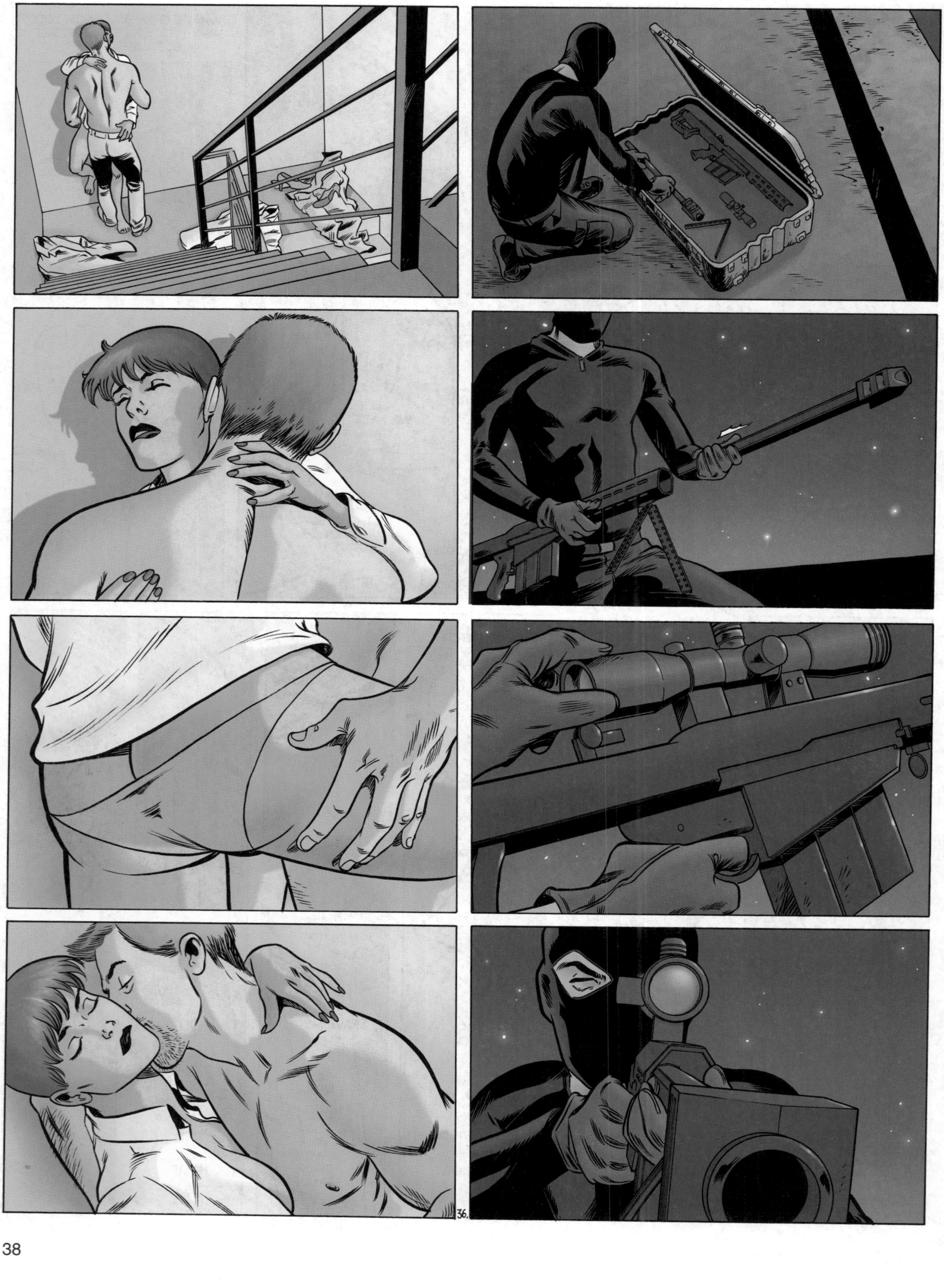
36.

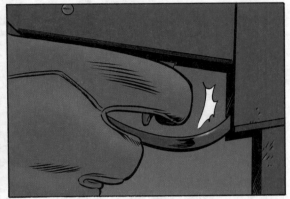

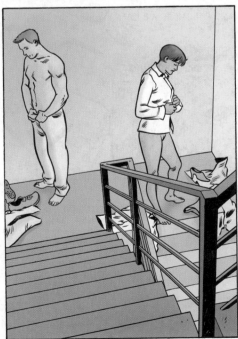

ELLIE, I...

DON'T SAY A WORD...

I'LL TAKE FIRST WATCH. GET SOME REST.

37.

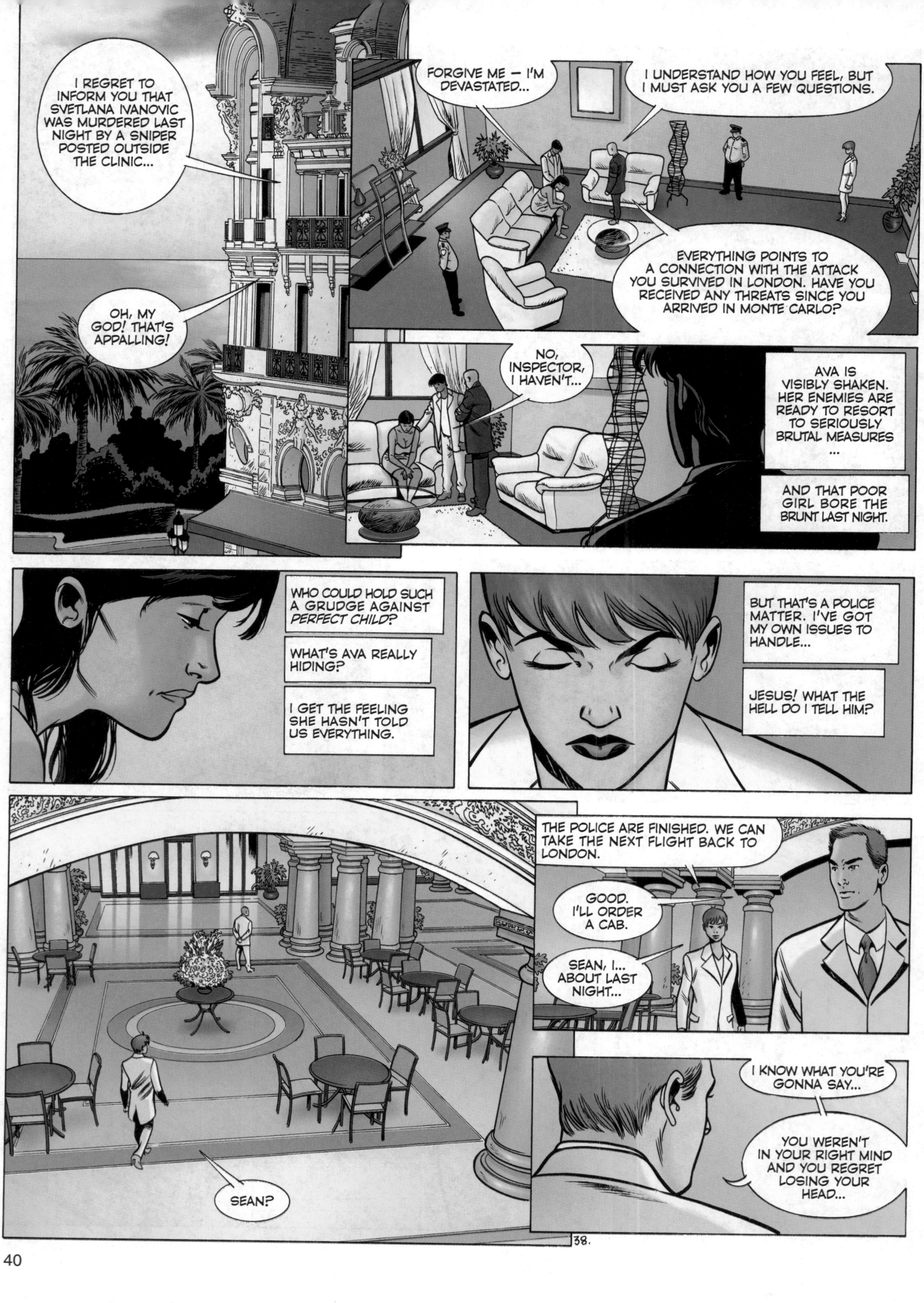
I REGRET TO INFORM YOU THAT SVETLANA IVANOVIC WAS MURDERED LAST NIGHT BY A SNIPER POSTED OUTSIDE THE CLINIC...
OH, MY GOD! THAT'S APPALLING!
FORGIVE ME — I'M DEVASTATED...
I UNDERSTAND HOW YOU FEEL, BUT I MUST ASK YOU A FEW QUESTIONS.
EVERYTHING POINTS TO A CONNECTION WITH THE ATTACK YOU SURVIVED IN LONDON. HAVE YOU RECEIVED ANY THREATS SINCE YOU ARRIVED IN MONTE CARLO?
NO, INSPECTOR, I HAVEN'T...
AVA IS VISIBLY SHAKEN. HER ENEMIES ARE READY TO RESORT TO SERIOUSLY BRUTAL MEASURES ...
AND THAT POOR GIRL BORE THE BRUNT LAST NIGHT.
WHO COULD HOLD SUCH A GRUDGE AGAINST *PERFECT CHILD?*
WHAT'S AVA REALLY HIDING?
I GET THE FEELING SHE HASN'T TOLD US EVERYTHING.
BUT THAT'S A POLICE MATTER. I'VE GOT MY OWN ISSUES TO HANDLE...
JESUS! WHAT THE HELL DO I TELL HIM?
SEAN?
THE POLICE ARE FINISHED. WE CAN TAKE THE NEXT FLIGHT BACK TO LONDON.
GOOD. I'LL ORDER A CAB.
SEAN, I... ABOUT LAST NIGHT...
I KNOW WHAT YOU'RE GONNA SAY...
YOU WEREN'T IN YOUR RIGHT MIND AND YOU REGRET LOSING YOUR HEAD...
38.

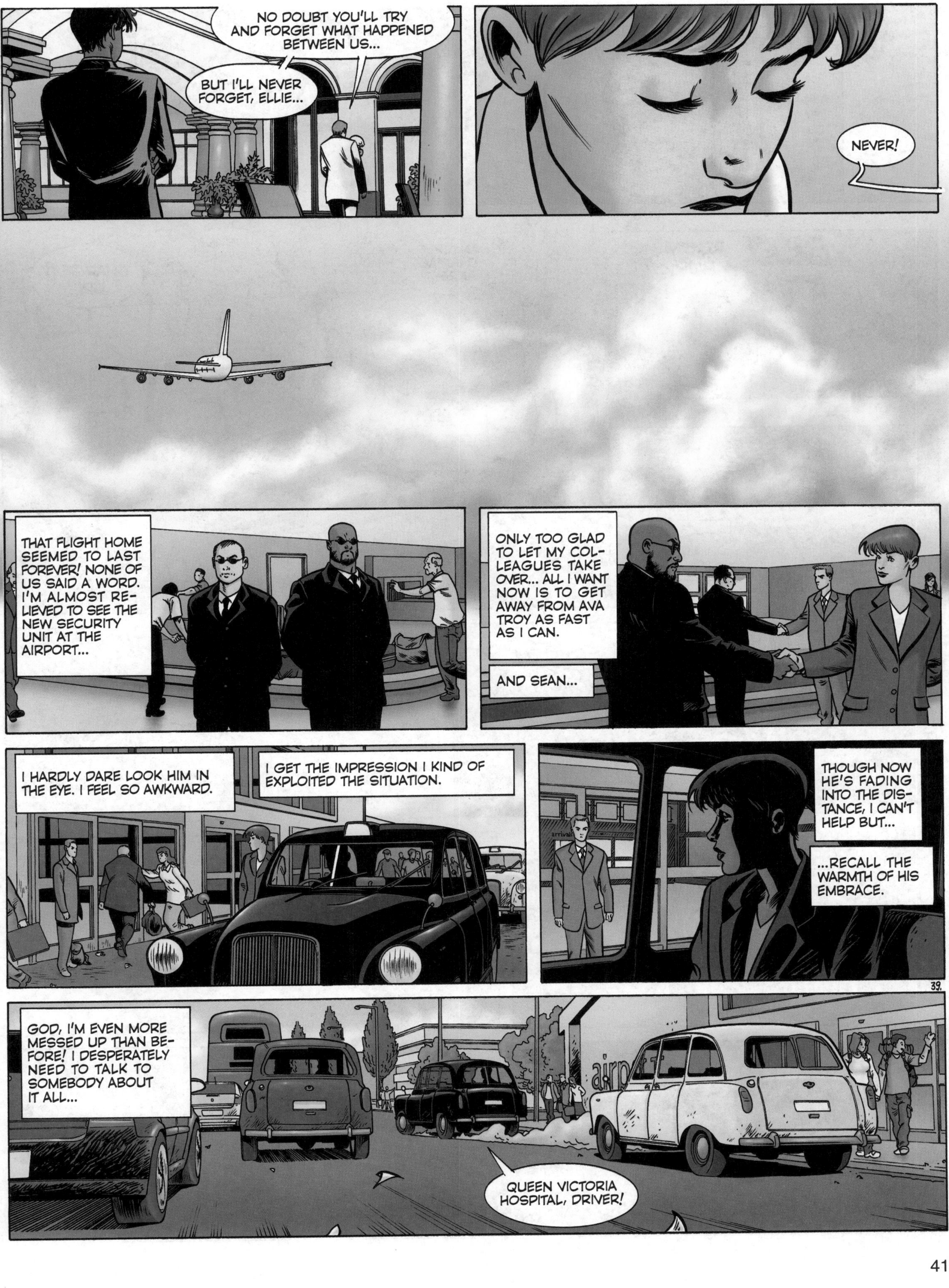
NO DOUBT YOU'LL TRY AND FORGET WHAT HAPPENED BETWEEN US...
BUT I'LL NEVER FORGET, ELLIE...
NEVER!
THAT FLIGHT HOME SEEMED TO LAST FOREVER! NONE OF US SAID A WORD. I'M ALMOST RELIEVED TO SEE THE NEW SECURITY UNIT AT THE AIRPORT...
ONLY TOO GLAD TO LET MY COLLEAGUES TAKE OVER... ALL I WANT NOW IS TO GET AWAY FROM AVA TROY AS FAST AS I CAN.
AND SEAN...
I HARDLY DARE LOOK HIM IN THE EYE. I FEEL SO AWKWARD.
I GET THE IMPRESSION I KIND OF EXPLOITED THE SITUATION.
THOUGH NOW HE'S FADING INTO THE DISTANCE, I CAN'T HELP BUT...
...RECALL THE WARMTH OF HIS EMBRACE.
39.
GOD, I'M EVEN MORE MESSED UP THAN BEFORE! I DESPERATELY NEED TO TALK TO SOMEBODY ABOUT IT ALL...
QUEEN VICTORIA HOSPITAL, DRIVER!

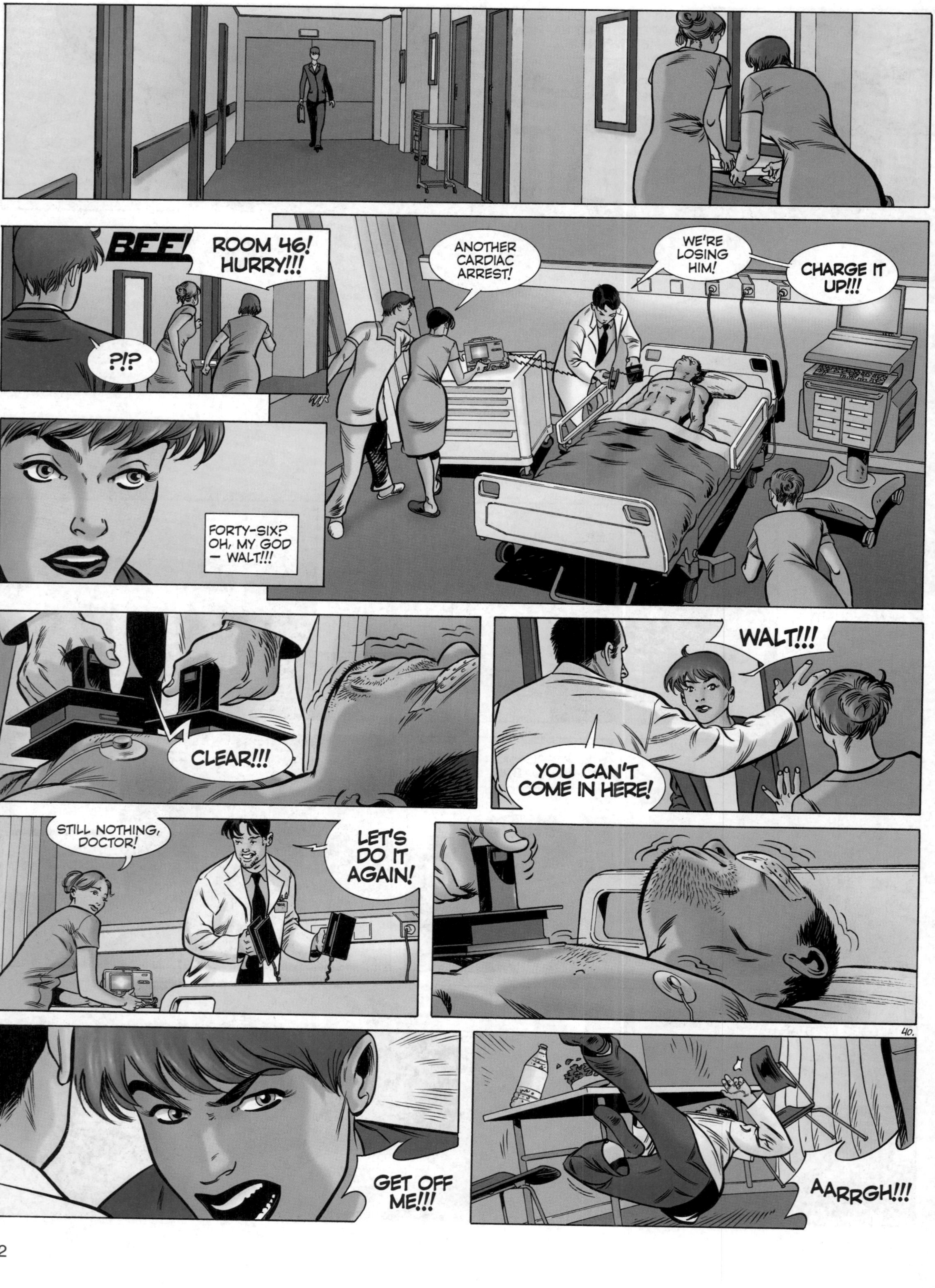
BEE!
ROOM 46! HURRY!!!
?!?
ANOTHER CARDIAC ARREST!
WE'RE LOSING HIM!
CHARGE IT UP!!!
FORTY-SIX? OH, MY GOD — WALT!!!
CLEAR!!!
WALT!!!
YOU CAN'T COME IN HERE!
STILL NOTHING, DOCTOR!
LET'S DO IT AGAIN!
40.
GET OFF ME!!!
AARRGH!!!

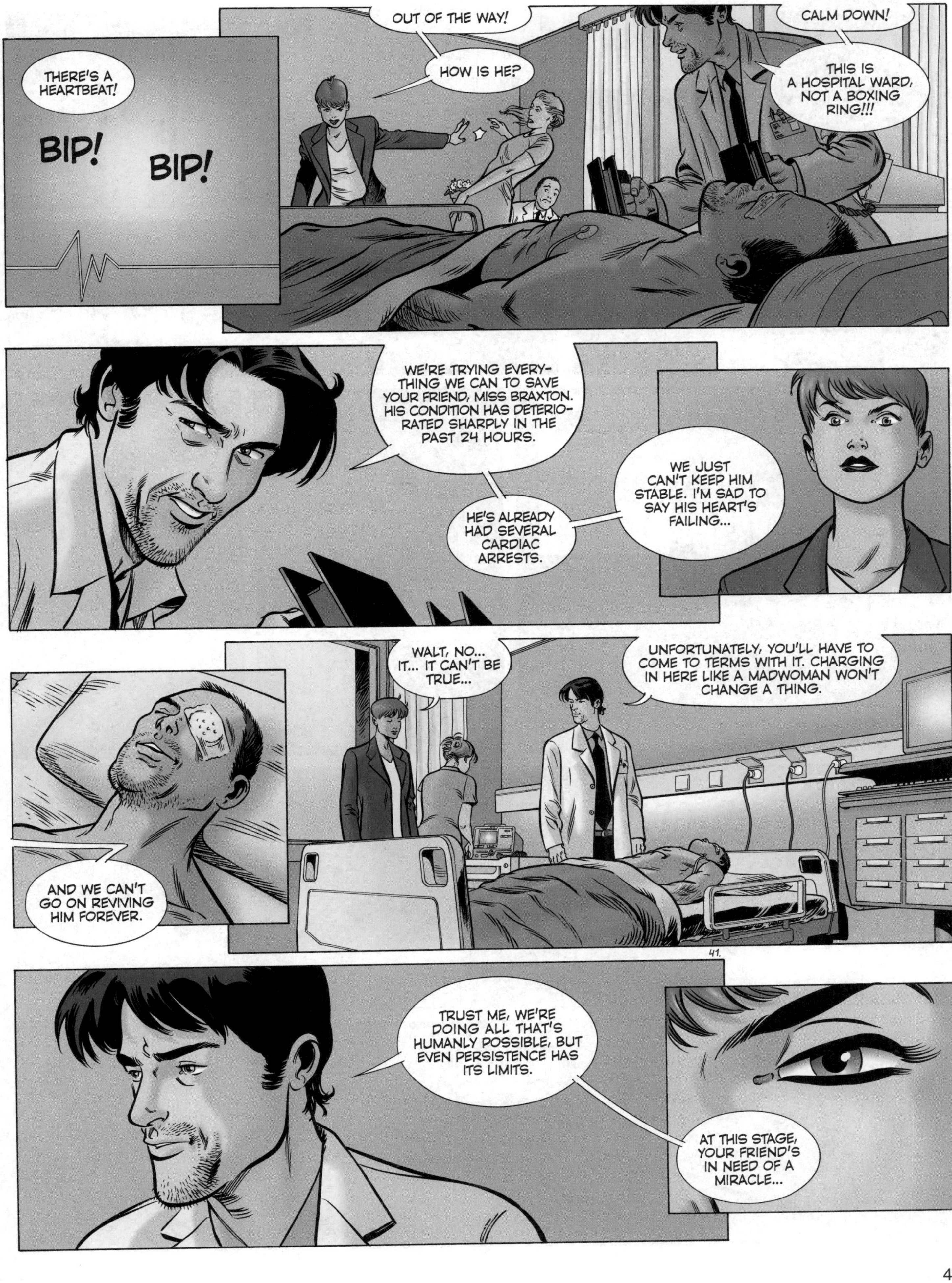
THERE'S A HEARTBEAT!
BIP!
BIP!
OUT OF THE WAY!
HOW IS HE?
CALM DOWN!
THIS IS A HOSPITAL WARD, NOT A BOXING RING!!!
WE'RE TRYING EVERY-THING WE CAN TO SAVE YOUR FRIEND, MISS BRAXTON. HIS CONDITION HAS DETERIO-RATED SHARPLY IN THE PAST 24 HOURS.
HE'S ALREADY HAD SEVERAL CARDIAC ARRESTS.
WE JUST CAN'T KEEP HIM STABLE. I'M SAD TO SAY HIS HEART'S FAILING...
AND WE CAN'T GO ON REVIVING HIM FOREVER.
WALT, NO... IT... IT CAN'T BE TRUE...
UNFORTUNATELY, YOU'LL HAVE TO COME TO TERMS WITH IT. CHARGING IN HERE LIKE A MADWOMAN WON'T CHANGE A THING.
41.
TRUST ME, WE'RE DOING ALL THAT'S HUMANLY POSSIBLE, BUT EVEN PERSISTENCE HAS ITS LIMITS.
AT THIS STAGE, YOUR FRIEND'S IN NEED OF A MIRACLE...

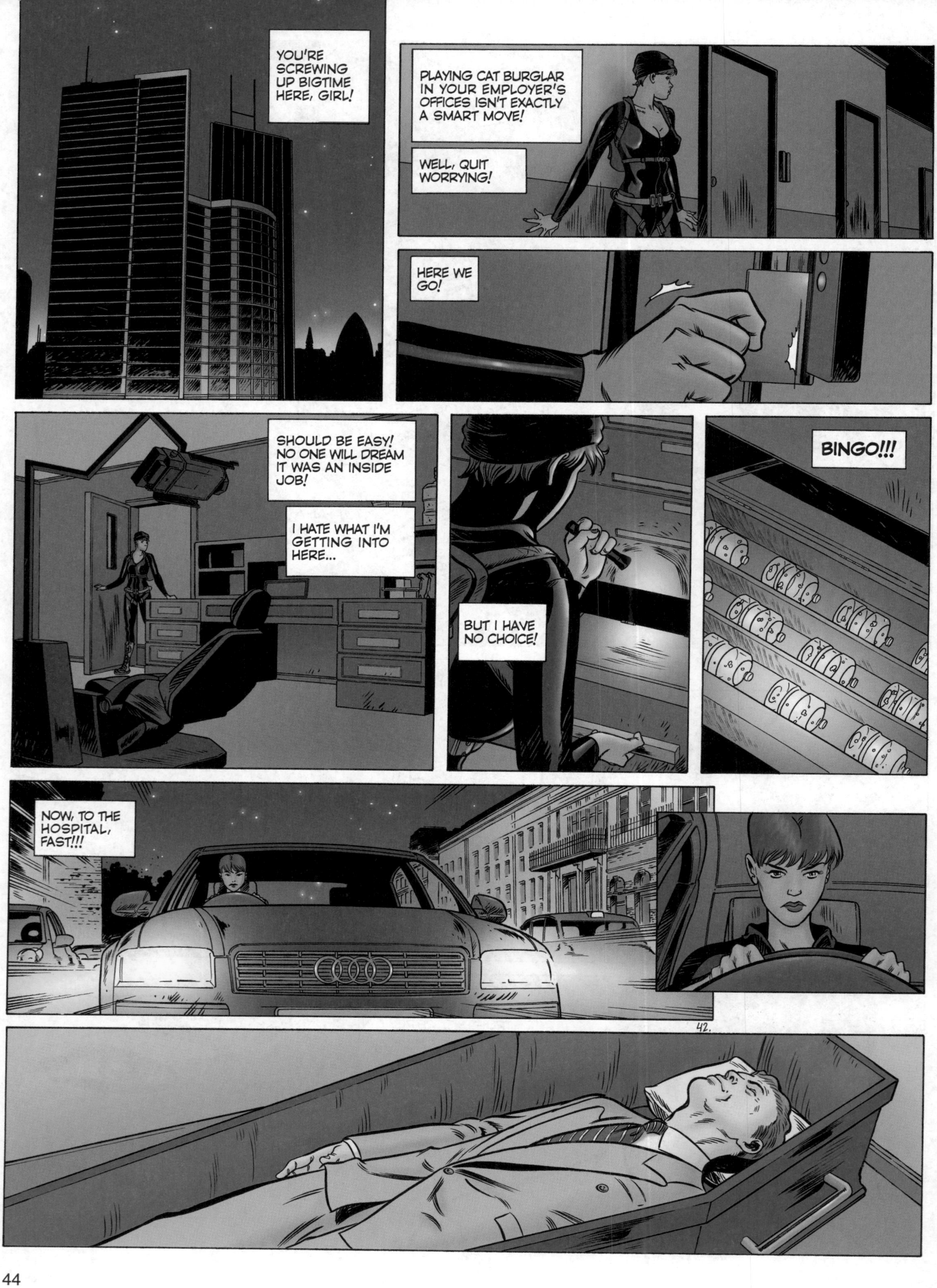
YOU'RE SCREWING UP BIGTIME HERE, GIRL!
PLAYING CAT BURGLAR IN YOUR EMPLOYER'S OFFICES ISN'T EXACTLY A SMART MOVE!
WELL, QUIT WORRYING!
HERE WE GO!
SHOULD BE EASY! NO ONE WILL DREAM IT WAS AN INSIDE JOB!
I HATE WHAT I'M GETTING INTO HERE...
BUT I HAVE NO CHOICE!
BINGO!!!
NOW, TO THE HOSPITAL, FAST!!!
42.

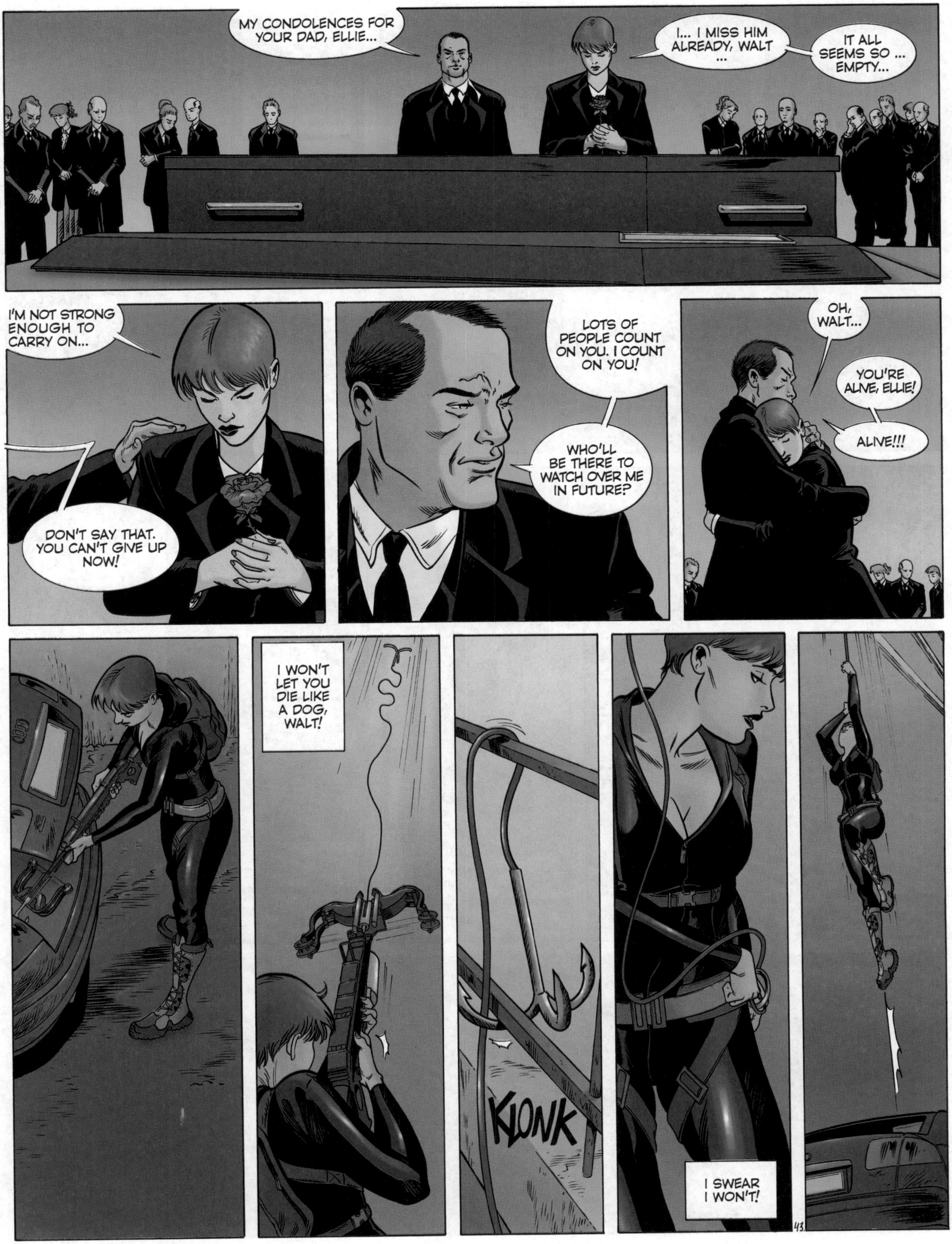

MY CONDOLENCES FOR YOUR DAD, ELLIE...
I... I MISS HIM ALREADY, WALT ...
IT ALL SEEMS SO ... EMPTY...
I'M NOT STRONG ENOUGH TO CARRY ON...
DON'T SAY THAT. YOU CAN'T GIVE UP NOW!
LOTS OF PEOPLE COUNT ON YOU. I COUNT ON YOU!
WHO'LL BE THERE TO WATCH OVER ME IN FUTURE?
OH, WALT...
YOU'RE ALIVE, ELLIE!
ALIVE!!!
I WON'T LET YOU DIE LIKE A DOG, WALT!
KLONK
I SWEAR I WON'T!

I KNOW VISITING HOURS ARE OVER, WALT...

BUT I'VE COME ROUND WITH A LITTLE PRESENT...

A TRIPLE DOSE OF 'BLITZ'!

SO, LET'S SEE WHAT THIS STUFF'S MADE OF! IT'LL EITHER SAVE YOU...

OR KILL YOU!

BUT YOU HAVE TO TRUST ME, WALT!

YOU WILL LIVE!!!

WELL, I'VE ONLY GOT ONE STAB AT THIS!

INTO THE HEART!!!

MY GOD, I... I WON'T BE STRONG ENOUGH...

C'MON! DON'T LOSE YOUR NERVE!

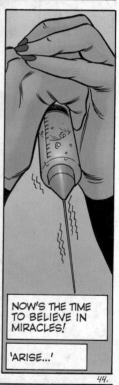

NOW'S THE TIME TO BELIEVE IN MIRACLES!

'ARISE...'

44.

'AND WALK!!!'

TUMP!

46

HHHHH!!!
WALT!!!
COUGH... WHAT THE...? COUGH...
EASY NOW, WALT. YOU'LL BE FINE...
WHAT'S GOING ON IN HERE?
E-ELLIE...
I'M HERE, WALT. IT'S ALL OK!
YOU'RE ALIVE!
ALIVE!!!
THANK YOU, GENTLEMEN. I SHAN'T BE NEEDING YOU AGAIN TONIGHT.
GOODBYE, MISS TROY.
EVENING, MA'AM. YOU'RE BACK LATE...
AN INTERMINABLE SHAREHOLDERS' DINNER... I'M EXHAUSTED.
GOOD-NIGHT, ALISTER.
45

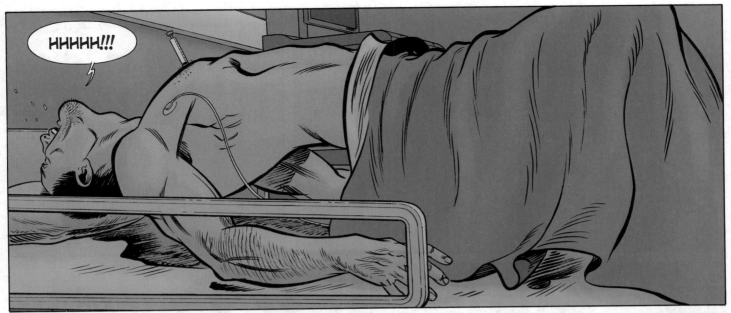

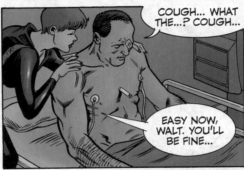

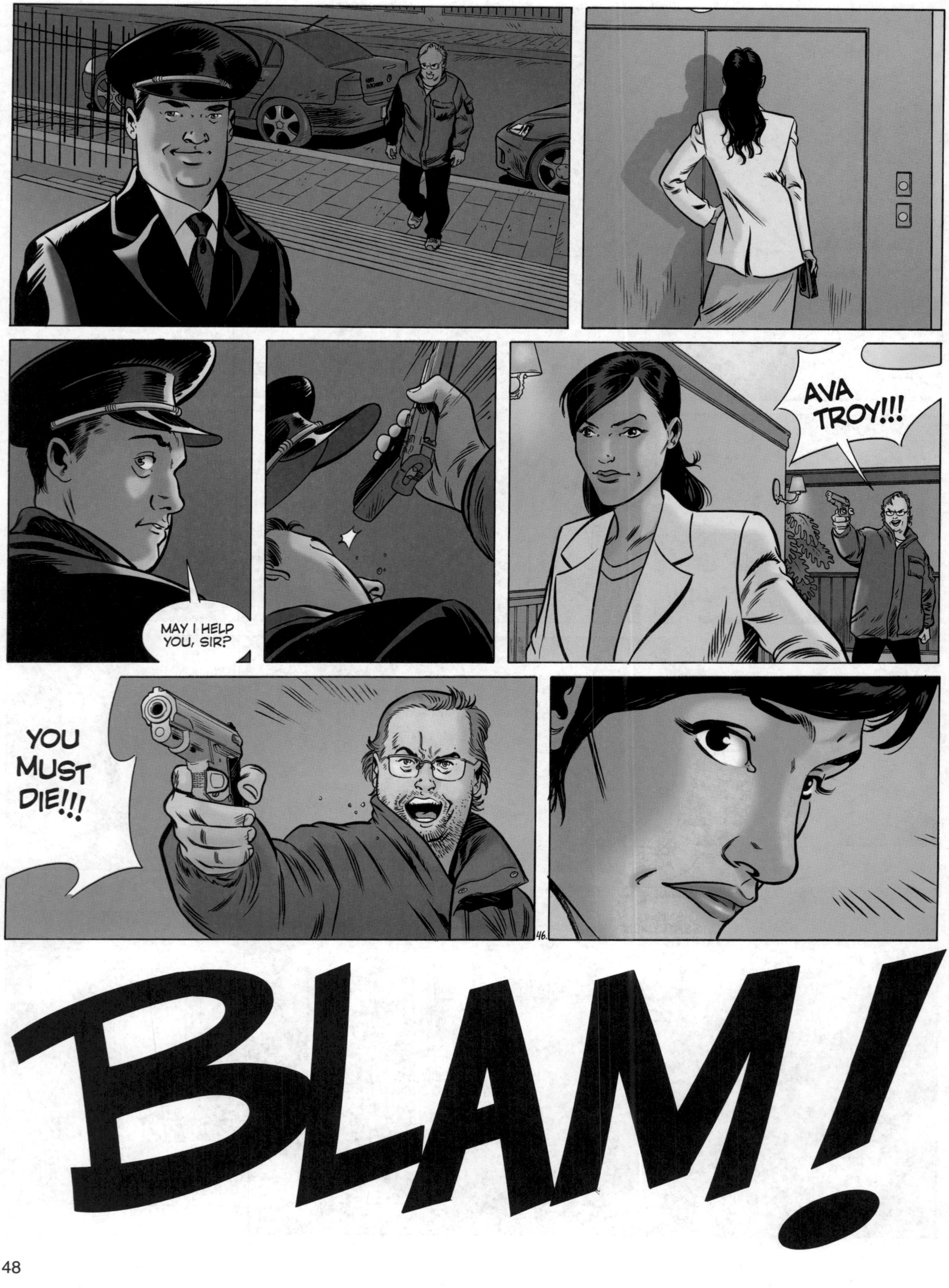
MAY I HELP YOU, SIR?
AVA TROY!!!
YOU MUST DIE!!!
46.
BLAM!